CHALLENGES TO THE FAIR SEX

Sarvasreyaskareem Sitam natoaham Ramaballabham!

I prostrate to Sita (the ideal of devout womanhood), the beloved of Sri Ramchandra and doer of good to all.

CHALLENGES TO THE FAIR SEX

Indian Woman: Problems, Plights and Progresses

Edited with

Introduction

by

J.L. GUPTA

GIAN PUBLISHING HOUSE
DELHI-110007

GIAN PUBLISHING HOUSE
29/6, Shakti Nagar, Delhi-110007, Ph. 7213053

ISBN 81-212-0041-5

Views, if any, expressed in the articles of this book are of the authors. The editor is not responsible for the same.

Printed in India

Published by Mrs. Gaytri Garg for Gian Publishing House, Delhi

Printed at
Bharat Enterprises, Delhi-110053.

Nari tum keval shraddha ho
Vishvas rajat nag pag tal mein!
Peeyoosha srota si baha karo
Jeevan ke sundar samtal mein!!

JAYSHANKAR PRASAD: KAMAYANI

Woman! you are mere faith in the silver mountain-foot of confidence. May you flow like a nectar-stream smoothening the beautiful plain of life.

DEDICATED

TO

MY REVEREND TEACHERS

AND

MY PARENTS

WHO MADE ME WHAT I AM

PREFACE

FROM times immemorial the fair sex has been evolving her own progress and development constituting more than fifty per cent population of the world. Undoubtedly she has been been combating several challenges. Womenfolk in India has facing the challenges in the forms of illiteracy, widowhood, sati, child marriage, purdah system, bigamy, bride-burning, rape, dowry, molestation, eve-teasing, etc. It was since long that the editor had been toying with the concept of writing something to depict these evils of the society against the fair sex. The outcome is the present volume containing essays by leading women writers in India.

The volume starts with An Introduction to challenges to the fair sex by the editor himself. The editor has put forth very interestingly the different facets, which are in one way or other, responsible so far as the upliftment of the woman is concerned. The various factors whether it is literacy, dowry, rape, sati or general neglect of the that sex, it can be considered impeding their growth. It is now time for a girl to be transformed as a reasonal girl to combat the menace of the day, concludes the editor.

The first essay being an attempt to highlight the position of Indian daughter-in-laws emphasises that they are still under chains as traditionally have been in Indian society. Ms. Hiranandani writes "World has reached the moon, but the

Indian daughter-in-law is still tied up by the rusted chains of convention and tradition."

Dr. (Mrs.) Bhoite, a very good scholar on woman studies, analyses the occupational problems of woman employees in rural areas saying that the role of these women employees is to act as changed agents, or to provide dynamic leadership to the womenfolk to change the entire pattern of life for a new kind of envisaged future. Since the cadre of women employees in the rural sector is created only after Independence, they are not accustomed to this role of woman. Employment of woman is to be socially recognised in Indian society.

Rape is another social evil impeding the progress of womenfolk, writes Ms. Premalatha. A crime is committed by men upon women, the men being the perpetrators and the women the victims. Section 375, I.P.C., defines rape when a man has sexual intercourse with a woman against her will, etc. 'A feeling of respect for a woman, for her body and her soul, should be created.' "Unless and until the fear of rape is completely eradicated, half the talent and energy is waste.'

In a talk in the All India Woman Writers' Conference at Ahmedabad, Ms. Bekkal says that 'The social sanctions and social limitations that are conventionally set against women writers have to be overcome with non-challance and belligerance. This they have to perform purely and exclusively through their writings.'

Dr. (Mrs.) Yasoda Devi provides a detailed study on the fair sex in Andhra Pradesh: the ancient history of the fair sex, medieval period and modern period in her essay in the fifth chapter in this volume.

Literacy which is of utmost importance to push up the fair sex has been given a very good treatment by Ms. Barua in her writeup: 'The need for literacy among Indian Women.'

Dr. (Mrs.) Prasad presents a research-oriented aspect of the tribal female labourers in the seventh chapter here. Women play a vital role in the rural economy of India too. But the disadvantages experienced by women in rural areas and their handicaps in becoming equal partners in development have emerged as critical issue in most of the countries of the world including India. She has presented beautiful data of the rural women being exploited in their working.

Status of woman construction workers in developing countries and particularly in India has been very systematically given the treatment herein by Smt. Gote-Garhane.

'Matri devo bhava' or Manu declares that God bless those families where women are happy and well treated. The ideal of Indian womanhood should be realised as holy as a mother. To study further the evolution of the feminine ideal in India from the ancient times, Mrs. Banerjee has come quite ahead in her attempt on 'Rediscovery of spiritualism in Indian womanhood.'

Evils in Indian society are the most crucial factors to have handicapped the progress of the fair sex. 'Prostitution as a profession is a social evil and is considered as a disgrace to civilization.' 'It is deeply rooted not only in India but also all the countries of the world,' writes Dr. Suryakumari in her paper on 'Prostitution: An Indian Perspective' herein. She also suggests certain measures to remove prostitution and to eradicate this evil from the Indian society.

Lastly, Dr. (Mrs.) Indira Devi gives a very comprehensive treatment to the status of women in Indian rural society. She presents the complete paper in three sections. Education, Technology, Women's Organizations etc., have been the main heads of her paper to analyse and explore the different challenges of the fair sex.

The editor heartly expresses his gratitude to all the contributors to this volume who readily evinced their interest and expedited their essays for inclusion herein.

Dr. (Mrs.) Anuradha Bhoite, Reader, Dept. of Sociology, Pune University has always been kind enough for valuable suggestions and the editor is highly thankful to her. Dr. A Suryakumari from Mother Teresa Women's University rendered great help in making this volume a success by asking Dr. (Mrs.) V. Yasoda Devi, Emeritus Reader in History, S.V. University, Tirupati to send her paper. The editor is very grateful to her, for the cooperation extended.

The editor is not less thankful to his coterie of comarades and well wishes as Dr. H.S. Upadhyay, Dept, of Philosophy, University of Allahabad; Mr. K.R. Dube, Calcutta; Dr. Bhim Singh, Sanskrit Dept., Punjabi University Patiala; and others.

The editor's better half Rita and his little Svasti Sri have been constant source of inspiration and they too deserve thanks.

Thanks are also due to the publisher who brought out the book in the best possible manner with nice get up.

J.L. GUPTA

X-MAS Day
25th Dec. 1987
24/30 Shakti Nagar
Delhi-110 007

CONTRIBUTORS TO THIS VOLUME

1. Ms Popati Hiranandani, Head (Retd.), Sindhi Department, K.C. College, Bombay
2. Dr (Mrs) Anuradha Bhoite, Reader, Department of Sociology, University of Poona, Pune
3. Ms. P. N. Premalatha, Lecturer, Department of Historical Studies, Mother Teresa Women's University, Kodaikanal-624, 102 (Tamil Nadu)
4. Ms. Nalini Bekal c/o Payipra Radhakrishnan Manary P.O. Muvattupuzha, Kerala
5. Dr (Mrs) V. Yasoda Devi, Emeritus Reader in History, S.V. University, Tirupati, Madras
6. Ms Kabita Barua, Dispur, Guwahati-781 006
7. Dr (Mrs) Sushama Sahay Prasad, Post Doctoral Fellow, Department of Anthropology, Ranchi University, Ranchi
8. Smt. Shubhangi G. Gote-Garhane, Lecturer, Deptt. of Sociology, Marathwada University, Aurangabad-431 004
9. Ms Jayasree Banerjee, 22, Sarkhel Para, Bally, Howrah
10. Dr A. Suryakumari, Dept of Ancient History, Mother Teresa Women's University, Kodaikanal-624 102
11. Dr (Mrs) M. Indira Devi, Lecturer, Dept. of Sociology, Andhra University, Waltair, Vishakhapatnam (A.P.)

CONTENTS

CHALLENGES TO THE FAIR SEX: AN INTRODUCTION

WITH the crack of dawn in a fresh day the eastern horizon looks to have started reddening and the clouds blushing in pink. The assiduous reader is up well glancing the headlines which look to have hogged nothing except the gruesome goings-on in different corners of the country. They fortuously do have a birds' eye-view of the matrimonial column almost replete with 'Decent match for a *divorcee* with no encumberances', etc. and the subsequent folios divulging a host of touching phenomena in the form of dastardly crimes with the weaker vessel. The highlights in different columns are setting a newly-wed ablaze, felo de se of a bride, rape, elopement, molestation, eve-teasing and so on. Virtually, keeping in view the chaotic environs and the utmost detterent factors responsible in not making a dent of centuries, this aspect is admittedly multiplying our national maladies by adding new dimensions.

It is an admitted fact that over the last four decades of India's independence the condition of woman has tremendously changed. The enthusiastic trend and the pluck among them to face the buffetting situation prognosticate the path of progress they would be paving in the offing by opening new vistas of achievement. In an interview with a noted Punjabi writer by Amrita Pritam the former continues—"so long as my body and soul do not snape into pieces, I will cry even before god" with a cavalier shrug of shoulder without once spilling a stifled sob.

Notwithstanding their efforts they are still far away from the status of equality with men granted by our constitution. The reason becomes obvious to find the percentage of educated women only thirteen according to 1961 census. However to overcome the sort of backwardness All India Women's Conference (AIWC) was organised. It was in 1955 when two bills on Hindu Marriage and Divorce and Hindu Succession were passed by. Pt Nehru. Smt. Sarojini Naidu, a symbol of India's awakened womanhood, did pioneering to emancipate the womenfolk. But a great deal is even today left to bring the weaker vessel on parity with that of the lords of creation.

Now turning to the socio-cultural milieu, since the Hindi term *Grihini* (House-wife) derives from *Grih* (House) and again denoting a sanctimonious image of the *Grih-laxmi* (the goddess of the house) it need not be assessed as the ridiculously abbreviated WIFE—to be spelled out as 'Worries Invited For Ever'. This ridiculous abbreviation does not at all seem to be having even an iota of element of truth. But the Marathi proverb certainly sums up an Indian woman's life in three words—*Janmalee, janmadeela, meli*—was born, gave birth, died. Anyway, whatsoever lies there, but one has to give consent to what Sakespeare declares—To have a bad wife is tempest in the harbour of life, but to have a good one is the harbour in the tempest. Further to pacify the curiousity of the audience the dramatist again evaluates a meritorious woman in his *Othello.* Enumerating the virtuousity and ingenuity of the fair sex he adds—a woman is meritorious who maintains her beauty permanently but does not take pride in it, has the power of speech but doesn't vociferate . . . sees many suitors pursuing but never turns her head in order to have a look at them and so on.

Even there is no dearth of appreciation in Hindu scriptures. It says that a better-half is instinctively imbued with qualities of head and heart in smoothening the daily life of her male consort. Narrating the six qualities consistent with the decency and civilized norms of behaviour it lays to the persevering reader:

> Bhojyeshu mata karyeshu mantree,
>   bachneshu dasee shayaneshu rambha !
> Dharmanukula kshamayadharittree,
>   bharyachakhadgunavteehdurlabha !!

In all the functionaries, she proves to be a mentor, happens to be a most affectionate mother in serving meals to her husband, beats in allegiance even to a trusted menial, excels even the celestial nymph Rambha in cohabitation and is meticulously imbued with temperaments, spiritualistic concepts, forgiveness and so forth.

Interestingly gone are the days when Satyavan and Savitri dwelt. The battle at Kurukshetra was fought as Bhima's pledge to avenge on Duryodhana by whom Draupadi was denuded. Rama decapitated the demon Ravana to let Sita preserve her devout womanhood. And Rama was heartly depressed on the eve of exile when Sita requested to accompany him. He forbade her to accompany him to far off jungles with her coquettish gait. It is how the great poet Tulsidas puts:

> Hansgavani tum nahi ban jogu !
>   Suni apayash mohi deihi logu !!
> Rahahu bhavan us hridaya vicharee !
>   Chandvadani dukh kanan bharee !!

Alash! now rapists are finding cancerous growth. Couples calibre is attenuating since loosing the memory of *Saptapadi i.e.*, the seven steps Hindu bride and groom walk together, making at the same time promises of mutual fidelity after which the nuptial tie becomes irrevocable. Contractors of law and order are seen exhibiting callous indifference and what to talk of public which is also displaying lecherous interest. Consequently the scant veneration of Vibhisana to console Sita undergoing pangs of gang rape, the turmoil of dowry and murder at Ashok

Vatika proves to be crying in wilderness. It becomes, therefore, incumbent on the woman herself to be conscious of the challenges whether of illiteracy, dowry-deaths, sati, wifebeating, rapes and exploitation in employment etc.

It would be necessary to examine in the present context the different facets responsible for the drawback of the Indian woman. Lack of education can be said to be one of the basic reasons. In order to recognise the schooling of girls and women in accelerating socio-economic development, the Government has formulated variety of measures from time to time and as a result there has been gradual but progressive increase in the enrolment of girls. The gap in the education of boys and girls is also narrowing down for the last two decades. There had been an annual growth of 2.8 per cent in enrolment of girls in classes I to V in 1980-81 and 6.3 per cent in classes VI to VIII.

Dowry which is a curse to the society has also caught the attention of law. The orders issued by the Government, Department of Porsonnel and Training, stipulate that any government employee accused of by the police of involvement in dowry death under Section 304B of IPC, shall be placed under suspension. Section 304B of IPC defines dowry death as follows:

> "There the death of woman caused by any burns or bodily injury or occurs otherwise than under normal circumstances within seven years of her marriage and it is shown that just before her death she was subjected to cruelty or harassment by her husband or any relative of her husband for, or in connexion with any demand for dowry such death shall be called 'dowry death' and such husband or relative shall be deemed to have caused her death."

In a book *Women and Divorce* by Vasudha Dagamwar the author concludes that things have not changed over the years. "A divorcee is damned as a scarlet woman" writes Promilla Kalhan, a seasoned journalist. Women are still given the treatment of third class citizens. Wife beating has always been witnessed among the conventional and narrow-minded villagers. May be they become lettered or unlettered beating and abusing is done on even slightest errors of wives. The author has been an eye-witness of certain cases of the like nature in eastern-parts of India. In urban areas and in metros too even the educated and economically independent ones like 'doctors, teachers and nurses suffer beating by their drunken husbands, swallow their pride and acquiesce to their men keeping mistresses or patronising prostitutes rather than call off the marriage' and 'a thief can go about a traditional Indian home freely than a husband who wants to sleep with his wife.' When he gets his opportunity he avails of it as hurriedly as he can leaving his wife sexually roused, unfulfilled and often pregnant, puts forth an woman journalist. An woman doctorate from London University has ultimately made up her mind to remain unmarried seeing the beastly Indian men's attitude towards the wives. As for the domesticated wives Rashme Sehgal comments, "These women seemed content to be wrapped in the cocoon of demesticity. . . . Many of them were pursuing old fashioned crafts such as needlework and embroidery." About marriage, a woman says, "The first few weaks of marriage are regarded as crucial because it is this period which determines which of the two partners will gain ascendency. The so-called honey-moon period is transformed into a trial of strength with both parties anxious to grab the reins of power. The woman, how-ever, does not display her weapons directly preferring to work insidiously on the gullible male through the weapons of sex, flattery and good food."

It is indeed shocking in the modern times that women are performing *sati* and are allowed to at the funeral pyres of their husbands. An 18-year old Rajput widow committed *sati* with the corpse of her husband on September 4, 1987 at a village Deorala in District Sikar (Rajasthan.) The Churi ceremony organised on that day was an ugly, crual manifestation of human degradation on the occasion marked with zeal and devotion. An 'element of superstition makes the exploitation of the gullible possible' but the law and order machinery should not remain inactive and deterred. The woman should not be allowed to finish at the alter of superstition. Social organisa-tions as well as the public in general should not be the helpless and silent spectators but they should take up the cudgels for uprooting the evils. In an interview published in the Hindustan Times the Deputy Commissioner of Police, Kanwaljit Deol, says: "Only Section 309 has been struck down whereas Section 306 IPC remains. So the crime part of suicide will still have effect. The British had added 306 IPC to prevent sati. Any assistance for it will be punishable whether it is a wilful attempt at self-immolation or a forced one."

Moreover, it is a great melancholy and would hardly suffice say at the outset that today's much-talked about dowry victims are being inflicted with severe agonies. They are hurled on sarcastical epithets or lashed on with obnoxious words by in-laws. In spite of the hazards of stringent sentences the receivers and givers of dowry are multiplying overnight. Do people apply their perceptive reason to the understanding as to where from the shortcomings genuinely emanate? What really impells a newly-wed girl to take the extreme step of pouring kerosene on herself ? And it sounds conceivably somewhat unreasonable to resort to and to blame in-laws and husbands as the actual abettors. Even the societal environs do not let them have a sigh of relief if they ever dare to stay longer with their parents when they seem to show disappointment with the in-laws and get involved in a dilemma of what to do. In that state of affair, is it not only the parents but the present social set up also which can be held responsible for perpetrating this evil. In these juncturous situations the daughters or daughter in-laws find no way out, neither given shelter with parents nor with society and it ultimately compells them to embrace the icy hands of death within the confinement with their Pati-parmeshwar (husband). Since the daughters are traditionally treated merely as one of the kiths and kins the very moment they get noosed in the bridal tie how far the things go well can be left on the populace itself to think over.

Further a thing of paramount significance which remains to put down here is to what extent the modern movies are successful in securing their objective. And which can be replied saying, presumably, no end of what is left in its aftermath. The present connotation practically becomes more conspicuous to witness the emerging generation clad in gorgeous and provocative dresses, which seduces their counterpart. Since my ears having been poisoned I cann't apply brake to recounting in a particular colony approximately a bevy of girls in their teens might have eloped away eventually seeking their nuptial tie in the court of law. Then what is actually contributing to such neumena ? On the whole and to fable not, the author does not cherish any biased trait against ultra-modern movies, materialistic nudity or the ostentation of the elitists. It does entail an emormous spectrum of beneficiares. But the butt of the argument is that that limits unto those who have developed high faculties of mind and can weigh the pros and cons of it. Conversely, it proves equally detrimental to the impeccable psyche of youngesters being on the verge of very *in precipio* of their life.

The entire crisis does not get at close here only. The *modus vivendi* (way of living) of the womenfolk in metros has relatively bettered to some an extent. By and by their status is improving to a new watermark from the very level of performing washes and operating in culinary department. If, perchance, one has a look on the *modus operandi* of a charred rustic lady, she is still looked differing redically from that of the urban one. Reviewing the millenium of annals of womenfolk in villages one finds scarcely any improvement till date. They can be still visualized ignorantly immersed in their hectic household activities. In the remotest villages these poor women are even today confined to servitude. Though innumnerable machineries are devised yet the doomed creature still have to winnow rice in a winnowing basket and the paddy in a mortar with pestle. The former is fortunate enough to be at large in going for lonely streches and fast living. But what else the latter finds in the four walls of house excepting to enjoy the juvenile pursuits of kids. No matter whether a mother is expectant or lectant she can hardly be rushed to hopital as being located in the farthest corner of villages.

In the long run I would be extending rousing welcome to R.N. Tagore's Aparna, a rational girl, to defy the domatic practices and oblations of Raghupati (*Sacrifice*) and to combat the emergence of the manace of the weaker vessel of the day.

J.L. GUPTA

1

INDIAN DAUGHTER-IN-LAW IN THE CHAINS

Ms. Popati R. Hiranandani

A PLETHORA of incidents is reported in our media of inhuman treatments meted out to the Indian daughter-in-law, like turning her into human vegetation by medical manipulation, burning her alive so forth and so on. In justaposition is the obnoxious behaviour of the daughters-in-law and an avalanche of anti-dowry laws and what not?

All this is the result of a single erroneous conception that "Woman's status is much lower than that of a man's." Usually an Indian groom feels it a favour to marry a woman. Due to this misconception he demands dowry and then the aftermath follows like a logical corollary.

A look around will show that a girl, after marriage generally becomes unhappy! Her freedom of movement is curtailed, her smile and laughter is turned into moroseness. She is treated like a prisoner or a slave. She has to yield to the high-handedness and arbitrariness of the in-laws. Woe be to the one whose husband also turns out to be an Ahmed Shah Abdali; And this happens in the houses where the head of the family doesn't allow the members of his family to breathe in the fresh air of modern ideas.

"Cover your head," "Touch the feet," "Obey us," "Take permission before going out," "Do not make any mention of your mother," "Forget your friends," "Do not read," "Cook and Serve", "Do not retort, even if you are provoked," "Your mother is bound to praise us under any circumstances," "You behave like the daughter-in-law of so and so," "So and so's mother has given this thing, your mother should also give the same." This is the only conversation with the daughter-in-law, albeit one-sided.

20th century is about to end, and 21st century is standing on the threshold with its hopes and aspirations, but the mother and father-in-law go on harping, "When we got married. . .". Not only do they themselves live in the past, but want to drag their daughter-in-law also thereby putting shackles on her feet!

World has reached the Moon, but the Indian daughter-in-law is still tied up by the rusted chains of convention and tradition—the chains being justified under the name of religion and morality! As if heaven is made only for the Indian woman and all her other counterparts are to go to hell! Suppose for arguments sake that this is correct, how is it worth to go through hell in this world?

The joint Indian family is the shadow of a clan of bygone days. The clan used to be under the charge of a powerful whose word was law unto all the children, women and youngsters. It is, therefore, that in some of the North Indian areas, as also in Sind, mother was addressed as Bhabhi (sister-in-law) and father as Dada (elder brother). Punjabis call the father 'Bhauji' and mother 'chaiji' (means Aunty or chachi).

With the passage of time the customs of treating the woman as 'challte' and daughters and sons as the ruled waned. In Sind the Amils used to build a first-floored room for the married son and the Bhaibands would furnish a small room in the yard and give it to the married sons. A Sindhi folk song runs as follows:

> Bring, Oh bring the doll,
> Adorn her with gold
> And put her to stay on the first floor.

Thus the married sons used to live separately, yet be one of the household without disrupting household unity.

But this sort of arrangement also led to problems like, envy among brothers, jealousy among their wives, elder brothers going away to distant lands, leaving young brothers and the young wives at home. All these led to the custom of separate house for the married son.

But this custom of separating the married son is common mostly amongst Hyderabadis. In other Sindhi communities the married son still lives with the father. Yet these days it is impossible to have a big household and live together. Today even a father finds it difficult to pull on with his own father or elder brother. He simply cannot accept anyone's authority. He calls upon his father and mother only during marriage or such other occasion for their guidance.

Under these circumstances, if he likes to rule over his son or daughter-in-law, it is nothing but an anachronism! This typing down by father and mother-in-law of their daughter-in-law in some customs and conventions in the name of religion and morality is highly improper in these days.

In fact, according to the belief of the ancient Indian religion, woman is an equal partner and companion of the man. She stands to help her man at every milestone of his life. Her status is not lower but equal to that of the man. If the husband is Swami, she is a Swamini, if he is a Deva, she is a Devi, if he is Vishnu, she is Laxmi.

But woman's status fell under the influence of Islam and in the process the selfishness of the man came to fore and in his lust for his own convenience and comfort he made her fall to such depths of degradation that the very definition of woman got tarnished. It is due to that definition that today's man feels it that he is obligating a woman by marrying her.

This misconception the mustard seed of all the social ills. The married woman should not try for a degree, nor for economic independence. That restriction is covered under the sort of "dignity" or the excuse of having everything. Bringing money through service has a value, whereas saving money through attending to domestic chores is devoid of all value. That at the most is bonded labour or hired help! Household work has simply become a lady should not go and work outside house, she finds a way of earning her livelihood and become independent. Women of rich families also harbour the same feelings. They jeer at serving married woman. This has been through centuries in the ears of the Indian women. Therefore, it is that many women neither themselves know the value of employment, nor do they teach their daughter or daughter-in-law or let them learn by themselves. This is the reason why in India one woman, *i. e.* the mother-in-law, becomes the instrument of harassing another woman daughter-in-law.

The daughter-in-law, when she crosses the threshold of her in-laws' home becomes the servant of a maid-servant (*i. e.* the mother-in-law) and the slave of a male-slave, (*i. e.* the son)! In some regions this conception crosses all limits, like in Saurashtra a father-in-law, who was to boot called his daughter-in-law to his bed at night. The daughter-in-law complained to her mother-in-law only to hear that "It is customary in our household. My brother-in-law and father-in-law also used to solicit me, hence you will have to comply." The girl revolted, with the result that the husband, brother-in-law and father-in-law burnt her! What a mockery of Religion!

On one hand the woman in India is considered a Devi, on the other she is compelled to become a Devdasi or married off and turned into 'Charnon ki dasi'!

It is due to such persecution that in some households daughter-in-law revolts and asks for a separate house. This is but natural. But when she demands to be separated she is put into disrepute. Is it a sin to wish for one's own home?

Yet in this changing society there are instances where a woman suffered as a daughter-in-law and again suffers as a mother-in-law. It does so happen that some persons have to suffer at both the ends, in a changing world or ideological revolutions. I know of such an instance in my mother's family.

Albeit all, the belief that woman is the husband's chattle must be immediately forsaken.

After all the daughter-in-law also is the daughter of some one. In-laws are no blood relatives of hers. That stranger has to be made one's own not by suppressing or putting restrictions on her, but through the process of love and respect.

My own sister's daughter is married to a Punjabi. But her father-in-law is God's good man.

My neice once made a car accident, and the car was smashed. She was scared to death that the father-in-law will be wild. She rang up her husband and narrated the whole incident and started crying. The husband gave the phone to his father, who just laughed and said, "Baby, you have made an accident! So now you can be considered to have learnt driving!"

Due to this exemplary attitude the father entered into a life time bondage of friendship with his son and earned a lasting place in the heart of his daughter-in-law. This father-in-law never even through mistake allows his daughter-in-law to remove his plates after meals. He is a very big Sethia. But if the servant does not turn up, he would himself remove his plate!

On the other hand I have the example of my another sister whose father-in-law throws invectives at his daughter-in-law and her father and she calls him 'a dog' at his back!

Speech has also got some civilised norms. To think that I am a father-in-law, and have a right to use invectives against my daughter-in-law and her relatives is wrong. That a father-in-law may go on pouring invectives and the daughter-in-law should silently listen to it is wrong.

Today everybody is enlightened. Today's father and mother-in-law are not fools as shown in 'Amrit' and 'Autar' nor are the daughters in law witches! Today's in-laws know it fully well that the flat is to be kept in one's own name and all the money is not to be made over to the son.

The best solution is to separate the son as soon as he marries. Let the son and daughter-in-law enjoy and bear the responsibilities. But if the housing position is as tight as in Bombay, one has to move in step with the times. Daughter-in-law is a human being. She is educated and knowledgeable. Therefore she should never be treated like a servant. The girl should also realise that the elders too have a status. If they do not behave improperly with her, she also should not comit the crime of treating the elders shabbily, in the name of freedom and excessive independence.

Let the elders set the ball rolling in this matter by treating their daughter-in-law nicely. One of my aunties had given the love of a mother to her daughter-in-law and she had not asked anything from her parents. In return the daughter-in-law treated not only her father and mother-in-law in the correct way but considered her seven sisters-in-law as her own sisters. Today she is the mother-in-law of six daughters-in-law but each one of them loves her like they would their own mother. After the delivery, she tells the daughter-in-law to give the child to her and take rest, as she must have lost her night sleep over the child. She prepares special strengthening fare for her. The result is that the parents of all her daughters-in-law simply shower love on her. That love and freedom are a must for a daughter-in-law, should never be lost sight of.

The mother of four well-known drama writer, Khanchand Daryani also used to give lots of love and respect to her daughters-in-law. Today her daughters-in-law are like sweet smelling flowers. Even to me, a friend of their sister-in-law they extend the sweetest of treatment!

Following in the footsteps of her mother-in-law, my aunty's daughter-in-law Sunita Malkani also makes the atmosphere fragrant with her behaviour. Thus good behaviour in turn begets good treatment. And it is the elders who have to start with the exemplary attitude.

In-laws should never forget that love begets love. Respect is a matter of give-and-take. They should get rid of the fixed notion that as daughter-in-law is a woman and a daughter-in-law to boot, therefore she is bound to suffer our tyrannies and it is her bounden duty to do our bidding.

Such notions, that in the modern age, cannot but bring in discord and revolt! Today it is the daughter-in-law who is burnt alive. Maybe a time will come when a daughter-in-law will burn a mother-in-law! Because action and re-action is equal and opposite!

2

OCCUPATIONAL PROBLEMS OF WOMEN EMPLOYEES IN RURAL AREAS: A SOCIOLOGICAL ANALYSIS

Dr (Mrs) Anuradha Bhoite

INTRODUCTION

EMPLOYMENT of woman in itself is a modern phenomenon in Indian Society. Specially in rural areas it constitutes a part of modernization introduced deliberately. Employment of woman as is understood in modern sense, in yet to be socially recognised in Indian society. To be more specific the rural people are not at all accostomed to this role of woman. They may be used to women labourers. But the cadre of women employees in the rural sector is created only after Independence. So, it is not surprising that the domestic setting as the accepted framework of women's lives, specially from the middle class, still underlies the pattern of woman's [expected role in rural India.

In such circumstances, the employed woman in rural area is bound to suffer from various kinds of difficulties which arise from conflicting demands put on her. She is likely to be torn between the two pressures working on her simultaneously—one to be a good housewife and the other to be an efficient employee. Torn between these two incompatible loyalties she is bound to suffer. In such a case the very purpose of employing her is likely to be defeated.

The cadre of women employees in rural areas was created only after Independence. When the Community Development Schemes were launched in villages for their all round development, women employees were recruited and sent to the villages, to work as gramsevikas, nurses and teachers.

Lately some of their problems have caught the attention of the people. Harassment of women employees in villages has been the topic of serious public discussion in recent times. A number of cases of harassment of women employees were reported in the newspapers and the same were discussed on the floor of Maharashtra legislature. Such public issues are always discussed on the level of personal opinions and emotions rather than on the basis of sociological facts. Such facts are however essential for a proper assessment of the situation and a sober evaluation of the different sides of the problems.

In this article an attempt is made to locate and analyse some of their problems.

METHODOLOGY

This article is based on my Ph.D. thesis entitled "A Study of the Problems of Employed Women in Rural Areas," which I completed in 1973. The locale of the study was Parbhani district of Maharashtra. For my research, I studied 163 cases of employed women who were working as gramsevikas, teachers and nurses. My sample included all these three categories. The data were collected by the use of well prepared structured schedule.

The main thrust of the research was to find out their different problems and trace their sociological causal factors. For the sake of the study, the problems of employed women were divided into three categories—familial, occupational and rural.

In the present attempt, we are going to discuss their occupational problems only. We have tried to show how their problems even of occupational category have emerged due to interplay of tradition and modernity. The entire rural environment is symbolizing tradition and their work role situation is symbolizing modernity.

NEW ROLE

The scrutiny of the data in my said research revealed that the employment of women in rural areas is a recent one. There may be a tradition of women of lower classes working as agricultural labourers. But women of middle class, coming out of their domestic shell, and working in villages, was certainly a new phenomenon in the villages.

The data showed 76 per cent of the women employees belonged to young age category *i.e.*, between 18-35 years. And 70.5 per cent of women employees have less than eight years experience in service. This emphasizes the newness of her role.

The new role is bound to create problems of adjustment for the women employees. It is always easier to play the institutionalized role. Because here it is easy to adjust with the expectations of the other. The shared beliefs, experiences, definitions of the situations and the criteria of evaluation make it safer for the actor to play the traditional or institutionalized role in accordance with the expectations of the other. But when the role is new, both the actor as well as alter are exposed to the ambiguous situation which leads to confusion, anxiety and uncertainty for the actor in the role performance.

When the role is entirely new, the actor as well as the alter are confused about the exact expectations from each other. The absence of such factors, as definite evaluative standards, values, shared beliefs and attitudes, make it difficult for the actor to cling to some definite behaviour pattern. Many things are uncertain and left to chance. The actor is left to unstructured situation. This uncertainty and ambivalence in the motivational structure of the actor and in the situation outside actor, is bound to give rise to strain and frustration.

In the present context, women's traditional roles as housewife and mother are more or less institutionalized. In India, girls are trained and socialized from the very childhood, for these roles. The woman is aware of her adult roles, so there is little ambiguity in playing these roles. But the new occupational role is bound to create confusion and ambivalence in the motivational structure of the employed woman, specially in rural areas. For different reasons, firstly, as the employment of woman is a recent phenomenon, she is not socialized for this role in her childhood. Secondly even today the role of employee outside the home is always considered as the male role in Indian society. So she is confused, whether to adhere to her traditional sex role norms or to the emergent norms of the occupational role. Thirdly as the role is new one, the criteria of evaluation, shared beliefs and attitudes, values etc. are yet to evolve. So many things are left to chance or to the individual or collective interpretation, bringing an element of confusion in the interaction.

That the new role exposes the actor to the insecurities and uncertainties is clear from the following illustrations.

> "As a rule it is easier to adjust one's behaviour to signals from other's conduct than to discern on one's own account, the relevant signals in a complicated environment."

Miller and Dallard illustrate this point with the following examples. It is easier to drive behind the vehicle of a friend to find the right way in a strange city than to fend for oneself even with the aid of map."[1]

Dr. Taylor too points out how it becomes difficult for one to cope up with the new situation. "New ways of doing and thinking always create ethical and spiritual unsecurities. Change automatically creates uncertainty about what is really happening and what can be expected. Furthermore, old ways practical for generations are likely to be considered as sacred."[2]

That the occupational role of woman creates problems of adjustment is clear from the following observation of Aileen

Ross too. She observes, "Each new occupational role taken over by women creates problems of adjustment of attitude and behaviour. The opposition to the people playing new roles, is caused by the uncertainty not only of the incumbent in the unfamiliar situation, but also those who played related roles."[3] This will be clear by the following illustration too. One teacher respondent in my sample said: "On many occasions, due to the exigencies of the work, we are required to stay long hours in the school. But if we stay for long hours in the school as our male colleagues do, it is not approved by our family members nor by the people in the village. If we neglect the work in the school, we probably get involved in the friction with the higher authority. It becomes then difficult to decide whether to stay at the school for long hours or return home."

From the above discussion it is clear that it becomes difficult for the individual to play a new role because of absence of any stabilized pattern of mutual expectations. This exposure to the new role is thus a problem faced by the employed women in rural areas.

DEFICIENCIES

The successful handling of any occupational role requires the occupant of the position, to have requisite qualifications, formal as well as informal along with other qualities. Let us examine this role of women employees in this context.

The scope of Community Development Programme was extended to cover the womenfolk of the villages only after 1952. This necessitated the recruitment of women workers for carrying out the developmental schemes. But initially the dearth of women workers having requisite qualifications was seriously felt for different reasons. One reason was that employment of woman was a new phenomenon. The second reason of this dearth was the general apathy and fear entertained by parents and guardians of the qualified girls to send them to remote villages. The third reason was that though the girls having requisite qualifications, were available in sufficient number in cities, these girls themselves were not willing to go to the villages, setting aside the attraction for city life.

Discussion with higher officers related with the implementation of the Community Development Programme, confirmed this point with officers like chief executive officer, block development officer and so on. The officers were unanimous in saying that there was generally a dearth of suitable women employees to work in rural areas. This was the state at least in the beginning of the Community Development projects. The following example will clearly reveal this state of affair.

The data about the educational level of women employees revealed that 70 p.c. of women employees have educational qualification below the matriculation level *i.e.*, below S.S.C. The minimum requirement was S.S.C. pass.

Another problem was inherent in the personality structure of Indian woman as she is brought up in Indian society. One needs to have certain typical personality traits for the proper performance of occupational role. As suggested by Dahlstrom "The successful occupational role is based on performance, effectiveness, information, ability, independence and initiative".[4] I think Indian woman in general and specially women having lower education, lack some of these qualities which are essential for playing the occupational role effectively. It is observed, submission and resignation are pronounced in Hindu woman's personality. Dr. Cormac observes, "Hindu women are submissive and that they do fulfil their potentialities or fully develop their individual personalities." She further points out, "woman is more member of a group than an individual, initiative is not encouraged, and there is a little place for it in the system. There is little social approval or encouragement of ambition of new ventures of deviant behaviour—— The general result is a compliant personality, and no other general type personality could normally develop under such social conditions."[5]

The role of these women employees is to act as change agents, or to provide dynamic leadership to the womenfolk to change the entire pattern of life for a new kind of envisaged future. As Dube (1983) points out, "The aim of C.D.P. is" "to initiate and direct a process of integrated cultural change aimed at transforming the social and economic life of the villages."[6] The aim of the CDP itself was to bring about attitudinal behavioural changes of rural women and create in them the need or urge for self-development. So the agents of change must have along with professional skills, the understanding of the fundamentals of CDP. It needs to be examined whether their training included the most needed approach towards development.

The other problem which was noted by the author in connection with these women employees was that most of them were not acquainted enough with the official procedure and formalities related with this job. Many women told that they were not properly oriented with such formalities as interpreting and drafting official letters, keeping the diary of the work, application for bills or leave complaints etc. Many respondents confided that as they were not accostomed with the male work world, they relied on male colleagues for such work. This also many times gave rise to anxiety and tensions as for women in India, mixing with men is a taboo. Kapadia (1966) rightly points out, "It was considered derogatory for a woman to take work outside the house, being primarily a question of social prestige and secondarily of involvement in the company of men."[7] Ward (1963) alludes to the same fact, "In countries, where the seclusion of women has been traditional, life is often exceedingly difficult for those few women who have merged into the man's world——An Indian or Pakistani woman may find this same situation for more difficult, the separation of the sexes have been traditionally so marked that there may at the outset appear to be virtually no respectable social pattern available for her and her male colleague to model their professional relationship upon."[8]

Some other problems such as occasional non-sympathetic from the superior officers, absence of promotions, unfair deal in transfer matters, touring job which disturbed the family life etc., were noted in this context.

Can we put in nutshell that her problems in the occupational field have emerged due to the confrontation of values of two groups which are diametrically opposite of each other.[9] Indian woman all through her life, is confined to the small primary group of family. Family embodies the values of particularism, diffuseness, effectivity and quality, while the occupational structure rests on universatism, performance, affective neutrality and specificity. Some of her problems can be attributed to the clash between these two group values or it may be worded as confrontation between tradition and modernity.

REFERENCES

1. Dahlstrom Edmund (Ed.), "The Changing Roles of Men and Women", Gerald Durkworth and Company Ltd. London, 1967, p. 45.
2. Dr. Taylor's quotation in "Indian villages in transition," Associated Publishing House 1969, by Durganand and Sinha, p. 211.
3. Rose Aileen, "The Hindu Family on its Urban Setting," University of Toronto Press, Bombay 1967, p. 200.
4. Dahlstrom Edmund (Ed.), "The Changing Roles of Men and Women" (Gerald Duckworth and Co. Ltd, London 1967) p. 47.
5. Cormack Margart, "The Hindu Woman" (Bureau of Publications, Teachers College) Columbia University, New York, 1953, pp. 199-200.
6. Dube. S.C., "India's Changing Villages" (Routledge and Kegan Paul Ltd. London 1958) p. 8.
7. Kapadia, K.H., "Marriage and Family in India" (Oxford University Press, London, 1966) p. 263.
8. Ward Barbara E. (Ed), "Women in New Asia", (UNESCO, Paris, 1963) p. 74.

3

RAPE: AN INCREASING THREAT TO INDIAN WOMANHOOD

Ms P.N. Premalatha

HALF of Indian humanity—the sisterhood of society has been deprived of self respect and is victim of a number of disabilities such as poverty, destitution, unemployment, unfavourable economic situation, ill-treatment and neglect, dowry and woman battering, sexual harassment and eve-teasing, above all the most cruel act of rape.

Rape is a crime committed by men upon women. In this act men are the criminals and women are the victims. Traditional view on rape is that it is an act carried out by men with sexual problems who are unable to control their sexual desires. Men are believed to have a virtually uncontrollable sexual desire which once awakened must find satisfaction unmindful of the consequences, and that it is a purely sexual act engaged in for the purpose of sexual satisfaction. But the feminist movement has altered the societal view of rape, and it is reconceptualised from a 'sex crime' to a 'violent crime.' Carol Smart views that rape is an act of extreme hostility and not a purely sexual act. It is a violent expression of hatred for women, not of sexual desire for them, though men achieve some kind of physical pleasure from raping women. According to June Hopkins, rape is a sexual expression of power and anger. It is motivated more by retaliatory and compensatory motives than sexual ones and it is a prelude sexual act complex and multi-determined, but addressing issues of hostility and control more than desire.

From ancient times to the present rape has played a critical role. It is a conscious process of intimidation by which all men keep all women in a state of fear. It is a symbolic means at some men's disposal of establishing power. The consequence of rape is so great that the victim will not reveal the event to others. Hence it remains an under-reported incident.

Since Indian society is a tradition bound one, incidents of rape has always been a rarity, even then there are references to rape in the ancient literatures. Though there are less cases of rape in India when compared to the West, still the act of rape is increasing fast in this country due to the impact of modern civilization and industrialization which changed the old conservative Indian morals.

More than 4000 cases of rape were reported in 1979 *i.e.* 12 rapes a day or one in every two hour.

(K. Murali Manohar, 1983, p. 24). The incidence of rape cases has gone up from 2487 in 1971 to 5023 in 1983 (S.K. Ghosh, 1984, p. 38). These figures can't be considered as a correct one, because very large percentage of these cases go unreported. In India conditions are so bad for a woman who reports rape and so the victims will not reveal the fact in order to avoid the humiliation and shame that is poured on her by the society.

Rape according to Section 375 of the Indian Penal Code is that:

1. a man has sexual intercourse with a woman against her will,
2. without her consent,

3. with her consent when her consent has been obtained by putting her in fear of death or hurt,
4. with her consent, when the man knows that he is not her husband and that her consent is given because she believes that he is another man to whom she is or believes herself to be lawfully married, and
5. with or without her consent when she is under 16 years of age.

There are two types of rapists. The motive of the first group is sex desire only. The other is motivated by an impulse to punish and hurt the victim rather than by sex desire. Gang rapes by dacoits, rapes on Harijan women, rapes on women during communal riots and other disputes, and rapes during war—all come under this group.

The punishment for rape is imprisonment for life or with imprisonment of either description for a term which may extend to 10 years and shall also be liable to fine, unless the woman raped is his own wife and not under 12 years of age, in which case he shall be punished with imprisonment of either description for a term which may extend to two years or with fine or with both.

Though laws are there in the law book for punishing the rapists, number of rape cases increase year by year. It reached its zenith during the Emergency period. Police raped a number of innocent women. In this context, it was not surprising that when the facts about the rape of Mathura, a young girl by two Policemen came to be known, there was a national outcry. When the two Policemen were set free by the Supreme Court, women from all over the country reacted angrily and the anti-rape movement throughout India was started. From amongst the number of organisations formed to fight rape, it was the Forum against Rape in Bombay, that expanded its activities to include investigations around specific cases in the area and offering support to the women. The Forum called for a boycott of all films that degrade and insult women. Finally the Forum organised a National Conference for women activists on various issues that concern and oppress women.

Whatever steps are taken there are still number of rape cases. It crosses all racial, ethnic, religious, age and socio-economic strata. Some peculiar kinds of rapes reported in newspapers are given here. There are many incidence of gang rapes, but at Pudukottai, a village in Tamil Nadu, a man around twenty-five years old raped number of women irrespective of age, caste or community. He entered the house with a knife and sword, threatened the inmates and raped whoever was there. By threatening, he prevented the village people from reporting to the Police. Unable to tolerate his atrocities, nineteen families left the village. It is significant that all of them are Harijans. One girl raped, by him committed suicide. Even infront of the mothers he raped the daughters and also even mothers. Other times he would hide himself in the nearby forest. Fortunately he was captured by the Police under 307 IPC and took action (Junior Vikadan, weekly, Madras, 3 December, 1986, also 10 December, 1986).

In another incident a man was murdered by his wife in an attempt to rape his daughter. The lower court at Vellore gave her life imprisonment. But she filed a criminal appeal to the High Court, Madras. The Bench said that the deceased who was under the influence of alcohal had no respect for morality and had gone to the extent of assaulting his own daughter with the intention of raping her. Inspite of the protest by his wife, the deceased had dragged the girl to the cot. The accused had no other go except putting an end to the life of her husband, to protest the modesty of the girls which they naturally valued more than the life of her husband and so she was freed (The Hindu, 23 July, 1987).

Manushi dated March-April, 1985 reported that at Wynad, a 16 year old dumb tribal girl was raped by the employer. She worked as a maid servant for four months. Then she returned pregnant, when asked about the pregnancy, she explained in sign language that the employer had come up to her from behind, when she was cooking and had caught hold of her. The employer is wealthy and influential so the politicians who came to the colony hearing the news of the girl's pregnancy were not eager to take up the case. Adivasi Sangam took out thrice a protest march to the house of the employer with the dumb girl in the forefront but the house was well protected by the local police so they had to return disappointed. The girl's father also gave a petition to the tribal development officer, but the authorities remained silent.

Another incident happened in a village called Babubigha consisting of 22 Chamar families situated in Nalanda district in Bihar. Recently Chamars who are landless and poor have been organised by the man in the village who is somewhat educated, to assert their rights. As a reaction, high caste men from surrounding villages sent them threats and warnings. A petition by the Chamars to the Police asking for protection received no response. On 10th June 1983, 45 high caste men entered the village beat up the men, raped the women and looted whatever they could find. Though the Supreme Court passed Orders favourable to the people of Babubigha, they are still repeatedly threatened by the high caste men—(Manushi, May-June 1984).

In Delhi, in January, 1984 three ten-year girls were kidnapped by two youngmen and they tried to rape them. One girl escaped and reported to the police. They were caught and in June 1987 the New Delhi High sessions Judge sentenced them to three years rigorous imprisonment and Rs. 1500 as fine, in default one year more imprisonment. (Thinamalar, 9 June, 1987).

Marital status is not an exception to rape. At Periyakulam in Tamil Nadu while a married woman aged 20 was sleeping inside the house, a neighbour entered the house and tried to rape her. She shouted and so the man escaped. She filed a case. (Thinamalar, 14 June, 1987.)

A saddest incident of rape happened to a married woman named Kamala Devi in Madras in July, 1987. Her husband's own brother raped her with the help of servant, and after that he asked the servants to rape her, but they refused. Then he killed her. After enquiry, it was found out that her husband only asked them to do so in order to marry another rich lady (Devi weekly, Madras, 8 July, 1987).

All these incidents reveal that rape is not only a sexual act, it is an abuse of power, and an act of violence and domination in which sexual activity becomes the means to totally debase and dehumanise the victim. Rape is an offence but rape takes place even inside police stations. The rape of Mathura by two policemen resulted in the anti-rape movement but even after there are rapes by policemen. On 25th 1987, *Indian Express* had a news about rape by a policeman. A young woman was allegedly raped by, a head constable, attached to the Srivilliputtur taluk Police Station.

A very large number of these cases go unrecorded. The reaction of other people to the female assault who fall victim to a sex offender are often less than sympathetic as fear of loss of reputation prevents the rape victims to report the offence to the police.

In the early part of the International Women's Decade, much attention was paid to the violence against women including rape. However in the later part of the decade, due to various factors violence is being challenged and rape is not treated as a personal problem but it is being discussed as a serious social problem.

In reality the rapist is not the respector of age or looks, community or caste and very often there is no other provocation for the crime except that the woman is woman. It is a manifestation of contempt towards women, an attitude which treats women as objects 'up for grabs'. All rapists are not perverts even normal men do rape. The rapist is not made in his childhood, but comes into being through a host of situational contigencies in adult life. Modern cinema, obscene literature, and dresses arose sexual desire. Sexual scenes are intentionally introduced in films though not necessary to the continuity of the story. There is hardly a film in which the villain does not either rape the heroine or make attempts to seduce her. Producers and Directors in the name of freeing individuals from social and religious restrictions encourage sexual acts.

Rape is a violation of a females integrity and dignity as a person. Fear of rape prevents women their freedom of movement; and are confined, protected and escorted in the interests of safety. Rape is a dishonour, a shameful thing for a woman and maximum social stigma is attached to it. It is a crime where the victim is the one who faces rejection and not the oppressor. The woman subject to rape is treated as a damaged property unfit for marriage, hence to be rejected. It is therefore no wonder that rape is the most unreported crime. Rejection by family and society drives many raped women to prostitution.

The obstacles in combating rapes are, the social attitude towards the victims, the police procedure, loopholes in the law, the criminal process, attitudes of the police, judiciary and lawyers, above all the family.

The law against rape has remained unchanged for many years. After considerable agitation by women's groups, a new Rape Bill was passed which amended some clauses, but did not incorporate the recommendations of women's groups and Joint Select Committee set up for the purpose. Legal and Police procedures are still very tardy. The victims find it difficult to undergo medical examinations immediately. Despite the existing legislation, legal redress is seldom sought by women because of their socio-economic status and lack of faith in law courts. The time consuming judicial procedures and the inability of the society to react to such happenings are more helpful to the law breakers, or than to the suffering women.

Many rape victims need support and counselling in coming to terms with their own feelings and in coping with the sometimes unsympathetic or unduly suspicious or morally judgemental attitudes of friends, family and interrogations.

The need to develop more helping services for the victims of crime is rapidly gaining recognition. A number of voluntary organizations, now undertake counselling and doing services for victims. The women's movements have alerted the police in order to prevent such offences.

Eradicating rape requires getting rid of power inequality between the sexes, because abuse of power flows from unequal power. Books, movies, television programmes must reflect equality between the sexes. A feeling of respect for a woman, for her body and her soul should be created. Men have to be trained to look upon her as a totality of spirit and body.

Television and film industries should reduce rape in their programmes. Children have to be taught that people who love them do not have the right to hit them, even for their good. Moral education should be introduced in all schools, where the sisterhood of women should be taught.

Public should be made aware of this problem. We must reduce the learned helplessness phenomenon found so commonly in women and replace it with assertiveness and equal opportunity among men and women. Boys and girls must be encouraged to become best friends they can. No doubt that rape has its root's in both family and society. Attitude of family and society towards boys and girls should be changed so that sisterhood can be established.

Rape, as an act of extreme violence is an obstacle for women's free movement, hence it prevents half of society's progress. Unless and until the fear of rape is completely eradicated, half the talent and energy is a waste. Women must be allowed full freedom of action and movement, and we small have to fight to remove this evil.

REFERENCES

1. Carol Smart, *Women, crime and criminology: A Feminist Critique*, London, 1976.
2. Carol Smart and Barry Smart, (ed) *Women, Sexuality and Sex Control*, London, 1978.
3. Elizabeth Whitelegg, Madeloine not, Elre Barteb, etc. (ed) *The changing experience of women*, Oxford, 1982.
4. S.K. Ghosh, *Women in a changing society*, New Delhi, 1984.
5. June Hopkins (ed) *Perspectives on Rape and Sexual Assault*, London, 1984.
6. Jyotsna Chatterjee, *The Women's Decade, 1975-1985: An Assessment*, Delhi, 1985.
7. Karabi Sen (ed) *Her Story: An Anthology of Studies in Women's Problems*, Delhi, 1985.
8. Lenore E. Walker, *The Battered Woman*, New York, 1979.
9. Marshall L. Shearer and Marguerite Shearer, *Raping about Sex*, London, 1982.
10. Mike Fitzgerarld, Gregor MC Lennan and Jennie Pawson (Compilors) Crime and Society: *Readings in History and Theory*, London, 1981.

11. Mildred Daley, Pagelow *Woman Battering: Victims and their Experiences*, London, 1981.
12. Miranda Davier (Compilor) *Third World, Second Sex: Women's Struggle and National Liberation*, London, 1983.
13. Murli Manohar, K. *Socio-Economic Status of Indian Women*, Delhi, 1983.
14. Neera Desai and Maithreyi Krishnaraj, *Women and Society in India*, Delhi, 1987.
15. Neera Desai and Vibhuti Patel, *Indian Women: Change and Challenge in the International Decade, 1975-1985*, Bombay, 1985.
16. Paripurnand Varma, *Sex Offences in India and Abroad: A Sociological Study*, Delhi, 1972.
17. Robert L. Sadoff (ed), *Rape, Violence and Responsibility: The Individual, the Family and Society*, New York, 1978.
18. Sushila Mehta, *Revolution and Status of Women's in India*, New Delhi, 1982.
19. Unlawful Sex: *A Report of a Howard League Working Party*, London, 1980.

Journals and Newspapers

William B. Sanders, *Rape and Women's Identity*, London, 1086

1. Manushi; 2, Devi,
3. Junior Vikadan,
1. The Hindu,
2. Indian Express,
3. Thinamalar,
4. Thinamani.

4

PROBLEMS OF WOMAN WRITERS*

Ms. Nalini Bekkal

I HAPPENED to be a writer, though not out of my choice or option. And that too, from the remotest part of our country.

What is really relevant to us in India, and at the present hour? Especially for a woman writer?

I have been, till this moment, contemplating this question. And I have found that the Indian writers have so far failed to adjust themselves to the international idiom of writers and artists at large.

We have only three sources to follow. The native indigenous folk idiom of our remote culture must be preserved without reducing it to a museum piece. Actually Jamini Roy, the Tagores (Abanindra, Gaganedra and Rabindranath Tagores) and the Neo-Bengal school of artists try to catapult their

*Talk by Nalini Bekkal in the All India Woman Writers Conference at Ahmedabad on 30, 31 May, 1986.

indigenous artistic idiom. But, then, that was during the period of our freedom struggle. To a large area and, may I say, to a great extent they succeeded in their endeavour in the early decades of this century.

If a writer in my village in Canannoore in Kerala is going to repeat the same experiment today, it will be disastrous. The exploration of the possibilities of the Thira or Theyyam of my native village, in present-day literature will thoroughly be futile. When I say this, I am fully aware that our Thira and Theyyan is replete with the deification of the primitive tribes through an annual spectacular ritual.

The second course of artistic creativity can conform to the so-called National or Indian tradition which may be called compendium of the various local streams configurating into the mainstream.

Again, the best illustration would be Bandopadhyaya or K.C.S. Panikker or Dilip Padgonkar or Amrita Shergil or Amrita Preetam or Kamala Das.

The third and the most powerful presidium is to produce works of art that suit the international taste of the present day. If as a writer, I write with a sensibility imbued with the problems of the third world, Women's Liberation, apartheid, anti-terrorism, NAM and CHOGAM etc. I am sure to be blamed with the callous disregard for my brethrenm. If the writers, conscious and sensibility are alive in me, I must be honest to myself. Conscientious artists like us have to be honest to ourselves. "Technique is Discovery," and that is the mark of originality as James Joyce put it. And Marques and his renowned critic Carpentier argue that Technique is Universal. Even Central African writers make use of Internationally valid technique to project their local, or indigenous or shamefacedly parochial themes.

So we come to the core of the question, the Indian, the local and the international moorings. How to synchronise them? Particularly since this is a time when the modern media like the T.V., Movie, Journals etc. have put us in a global village. Excuse me for employing Marcuse' phrase "The Global Village" or Schumarker's "Small is Beautiful."

The social sanctions and social limitations that are conventionally set against Woman Writers have to be overcome with nonchallance and belligerance. This they have to perform purely and exclusively through their writings, because and if they happened to be writers. Even the weakest writers emerging from the weaker sex are facing the problems and confronting the same conflicts as the strongest of the writers belonging to the male tribe.

I only put up a question in the belief that a writer in India, peculiarly a woman writer in Kerala can see purely theoretical and ideational anchorage from an august audience of a national dimension.

5

WOMEN IN ANDHRA PRADESH

DR (MRS) V. YASODA DEVI

INTRODUCTION

THE fair sex constituting half the population of the world, in evolving its own full fledged growth and development through the ages, had to tackle innumerable challenges in the form of several afflictions largely from the male sex. These afflictions varied from continent to continent and country to country due to differences in natural environment, climate, race, history and culture. India, one of the most ancient civilised nations in the world, is rightfully proud of a glorious past and bright and promising future. Indian women had to face many challenges through the centuries, as history reveals, some in common with women in other countries but many peculiar to their motherland, India. The afflictions were in the form of sex, caste, illiteracy, child marriage, widowhood, sati, bigamy etc. leading to social and religion's inhibitions and economic dependence of the aggrieved categories. Most poignant is the fact that even the children of such unfortunate women were victims of the problems faced by their mothers. These challenges were met by women of the various regions of the country in different ways to suit their peculiar problems but with striking and significant similarities to project the redeeming feature of the Indian subcontinent *viz.* 'Unity in Diversity.' Women in Andhra Pradesh were no exception to this.

ANDHRADESA

A considerably more extensive area than Andhra Pradesh, Andhradesa, was a distinct linguistic region of the Telugu speaking people in Eastern Dekkan extending upto the Mahanadi (now in Orissa). Andhra Pradesh ranks fifth in extent and fourth in population and second in language, next only to Hindi, with more than five crores of Telugu speaking people. With rich potential resources and minerals dependant on the bounty of nature in the perennial rivers—Godavari, Krishna and Pennar—resulting in the sequence of the deltaic systems of the rivers from north to south in the coastal region and the huge thanks in Telangana and Rayalaseema, render Andhra Pradesh fertile and prosperous as visualised in the Telugu Anthem (Ma Telugu Talliki) and the song 'Navodayam' portraying Mother Andhra just as 'Janaganaman' and 'Vandemataram' depict mother India.

Though geographically in three regions, historically Andhradesa had the fourth region of Kalinga, the southern part of present state of Orissa. The Andhras were an ancient people figuring in Aitareya Brahmana and Andhra history specifically starts with the Andhra Satavahanas in the 3rd Century B.C. The Ikshvakus and the Pallavas were the political successors of the Satavahanas and in their turn were supplanted by the Vishnu Kundins and the Salankayanas. The Eastern Chalukyas, like the Satavahanas had a long rule for more than four centuries and paved the way for the emergence of the Kakatiyas to power constituting the most formative age in Andhradesa. Theirs was the third successive Empire in Andhradesa, the two earlier empires being the Satavahana and the Eastern Chalukya respectively. The Kakatiya Empire fell a victim to the wrath of the Muslims—the Khiljis and the Tugjluks; resurgence and Hindu revival was the work of the Musunuri Nayaks and the Reddis. The Reddi rule of a Century and half marks efflourescence of Andhradesa which was transformed into Mahitandhradesa and Mahaniyandhradesa, that is, glorious Andhra as mentioned in inscriptions. Andhra trade and culture extended into South East Asia in this period, a phenomenon which prevailed in the Satavahana period. Thus Greater Andhra was visualised. The Rayas of Vijayanagar and the Gajapathis were the political successors of the Reddis. As part of Vijayanagar Empire, Andhradesa had its share of the benefits of the rule of the Rayas, particularly in culture, art and architecture. The close of the Vijayanagar rule marks the close of the medieval period in Andhra history and the dawn of early modern Andhra.

THE SATAVAHANA EMPIRE

Women in this glorious and Golden Age of South Indian history, especially those of higher social strata, could rise above the afflictions of sex, caste and class and distinguish themselves in the areas of politics, administration, religion and literature by their beneficial activities. In these services, they were on par with women in North India in vedic and contemporary Maurya and Sunga periods.

(*a*) *Nomenclature*—A unique feature of Andhra women, with no parallel in contemporary North India, attesting to their predominance and power, prestige and honour is that their names were prefixed to the names of their sons. This political convention—matrilineal names—speaks of the boldness and personality of the women of the royal families and aristocratic society. How far this feature infiltrated the lower strata of society is not very specific *e.g.* Gautamputra Satakarni (AD 78-102), Vasishtiputra Pulamavi, Matharipurtra Sakasena, Bhojaki, Mahabhojaki, Mahasenapatini, Senapatini, Mahakalavarini and Talavarini were the female designations of these cadres of officers.

(*b*) *Administration*—The keen interest and participation of the Satavahana Queens and Princesses in Imperial and State affairs shows how they could get training in political economy along with their compeers, the Princes and Rulers. For example (1) Devi Nagarika, Queen of Satakarni I (BC 180-170) and daughter of Maharathi Trinakairo, a local ruler in Maharashtra had profound influence on her husband and his victorious achievements. Her administration of the kingdom during the regime of Vedisri, one of her sons is suggested by the celebrated Nanaght inscription. (2) Gautami Balasri, the Queen of Sivasvati Maharaja, mother of Gautamiputra Satakarni and grandmother of Pulamavi was the motive power guiding the administration for three generations—self, son and grandson. (3) Maharani Vasishti Devi, Queen of Gautamiputra Satakarni and daughter-in-law of Gautami Balasri and mother of Pulamavi is credited with laudable qualities and strong will power by the Nasik inscription.

(*c*) *Religion*—That women of the higher strata of society wherein the caste system was not rigid and mobility was possible, could follow their own religion and make substantial donations shows their spiritual freedom and economic independence. Devi Nagarika performed two Asvamedhas, one Rajasuya and several other sacrifices with her husband and gave plenty in charity. Gautami Balasri, besides making substantial grants with her husband, son and grandson, on her own excavated a cave-vihara for the Buddhist monks *i.e.* Bikshus. Subsequently Vasishtidevi built a cave monastery on Tiranvu hill for the Bikshus and donated a village for its maintenance. As that village was not duly cultivated by the donees, she ordered the king's officer at Govardhanahara (Province) to implement her further gift of lands from the royal domain. The officer, in his turn, while following the Queen's command affectionately enquires about her welfare. This shows the Queen's hold on the kindom and popularity winning the gratitude and love of the subjects, perhaps more than the king. Almost all the Satavahana monuments, Buddhistic, were raised by women and endowed by them, Vishnudatta, a Saka woman donated 3500 karshapanas to the Buddhist sangha at Nasik. Women of middle class in society did not lag behind the royal and rich ladies in their religious fervour and economic position exemplified in their raising of edifices or making donations to Buddha and Buddhistic order respectively. The innumerable Ayaka pillars profusely sculptured, toranas, basements of the stupas in Amaravati were the work of women devotees. The Chaityas in Nasik and Kuda were built by women. They had a significant role in the construction of the Karla Chaitya of international fame. Women made magnificent gifts to these monuments.

(*d*) *Literature*—The challenges of illiteracy and ignorance leading to the relegation of women into lethargy and immorality were overcome by higher education and study of Dharmasastras, and literature. Women were boldly participating in literary contests and religious discourses on par with learned scholars in royal court and public discussions. Queen Malayavaki had a major role in the compilation of Gathasaptasati in prakrit by her husband King Hala entitled Kavivatsala. In this highly erotic work comprising 700 gathas, quite a good number were composed by poetesses namely Anulabdhi, Anulakshmi, Reva, Prahata, Vardhavati, Sasiprabha, and Madhavi. The high calibre of the style and substance of the work are evident from the saying "Amritam Prakritam Kavyam". The amorous life of Princess Lilavati, daughter of Sitamegha of Simhala *i.e.* Sri Lanka with King Hala was the theme of Lilavati Kavya in Prakrit by kavi Kutuhala. The Princess was residing at Saptagodavaram *i.e.* Draksharama. The legend that Malayavati's ridicule of Hala while immersed in jalakrida resulted in his learning of Sanskrit within six months shows that women were adept in several languages.

(*e*) *Education*—Lack of education among women was tackled successfully by novices of Buddhist order known as Saminikas, Pavajitikas and Bikshunis. These categories of Sanyasins were introduced to learning by preceptors or teachers mentioned as Uphajhayayis. The teachers gave instruction to girls of affluent families. Some of the Bikshunis were grihasthas, (*f*) *Fine Arts*—The high intellectual attainments of women in music, dance and painting, more than of men are revealed in the sculptures of the Satavahana monuments besides contemporary literature. The scene of two women engaged in playing vina in a sitting posture and dancing respectively in the larger panel of 'quarrel for the relics of Buddha' in a sculpture at Amaravati shows that talented women acquired expertise in instrumental music and natya, possibly of Bharata or Kuchipudi. The lifelike images of men and women seated on elephants standing on their knees at Karla attest the adventurous spirit, valour and martial vigour of the Satavahana women of higher classes. The images of two women standing holding paraphernalia of worship on either side of a gateway, a Buddhist relic in Dhanabodu neat Jaggayyapata imply the intensity of adoration to Buddha in this period. The sculptures of mithunas at Goli mirror the rich costumes, jewellery and embellishments of contemporary women in Andhradesa. The dressing of hair by women in plaits and ties *e.g.* Jata and Dhammilla in a variety of ways and vivacious decoration of them from the sculptures at Amaravati, Ajanta and Sanchi has strong resemblance with the hair dressing of women of Indus culture. The Sairandhris specially trained in the art of decoration were employed in palaces and rich mansions. Many types of jewels of women are known from sculptures. Vatsayana in Kama Sastra, a contemporary work mentions the ganikas or vesyas learned in the 64 arts. This category of women, the progeny of anuloma and pratiloma marriages, had to face the affliction of heinousness, repulsion and untouchability and were able to overcome the stigma by their learning, particularly in music and dance. They participated in the festivals—yaksharatri, kaumudijagaram, madanotsavam and sahakarabhanjakam, popular in this age.

THE IKSHVAKUS AND THEIR SUCCESSORS

More than the women of the Satavahana Empire, the women in the Ikshvaku period in Andhradesa were more confident and assertive in meeting the challenges to their position, power and prestige at different levels in political, religious, literary and social spheres.

(*a*) *Nomenclature*—As in the Satavahana period, the method of matrilineal nomenclature of king was adopted attesting to the high status of royal ladies. The name of Vasishtiputra Sri Santamula of the first Ikshvaku ruler shows that his mother was Vasishti. The next ruler was Mandhariputra Sri Virapurushadatta. His mother was Mandhari *i.e.* Mathari. Similarly, the names of feudatory rulers *e.g.* Vasishtiputra Skandasri of Pugiya family and Skandavisakha of Dhanaka lineage imply the powerful position of the mother in a family in general in this period.

(*b*) *Administration*—Women had profound influence in the politics of the kingdom, internal rule as well as external affairs. The diplomatic matrimonial alliances with local magnates and other kingdoms attest this phenomenon. Santimula's sisters Santisri and Harmyasri were married into Pugia and and Dhanaka houses. Mahadevi Rudrabhattarika, the queen of Virapurushadatta was the daughter of Rudrasena (AD 199-233) Ujjayini. Their daughter Princess Kodabalisiri was the queen of the ruler of Chutukula of Banavasi (Vaijayanti). Women bore titles indicating their status *e.g.* Santisri's titles were Mahasamanta, mahatalavarini and mahadanapatni. The cross cousin marriages were prevalent in this period *e.g.* Three queens of Virapurushadatta were his nieces.

(*c*) *Religion*—The unique feature of the women of this age, more predominant than in the Satavahana Empire, was their religious freedom. It is quite interesting that the kings and princes and other cadres of men were adoring Hindu pantheon but the queens, princesses and ladies of noble families were staunch Buddhists. Though Vasishti and Mandhari had their share in Santamula's performance of Asvamedha, Agnistoma, Agnihotra and Vajapeya sacrifices and gift of crores of gold coins, lakhs of cows, ploughs and land, as mentioned in inscriptions, their devotion and that of other royal ladies materialised in the construction of the Maha Chaitya at Nagarjunakonda, now preserved on Nandikonda. The Nagarjunakonda Bauddha-vihara in the Nagarjunakonda valley rendered holy by the residence of Nagarjunacharya, the founder of the Madhyamika form of Buddhism, which soaked Andhradesa, acquired global fame. The magnanimous ladies not merely raised the Mahachaitya as a complex but made sustantial grants for its maintenance testifying their sound economic position. The Mahachaitya and the profusion of sculptures attest the continuance of the Amaravati style of art in the 3rd and the 4th stage of development. The sculptures show the final stage in the construction of the prakara of Amaravati Mahachaitya. They are superb in the depiction of postures, poses and depiction of the human body. Princess Kodabalisiri built a vihara at Nagarjunakonda.

(*d*) *Literature and Fine Arts*—The women of the period were not merely charitable and pious but were learned. 'Panditastrilu' *i.e.* scholar women are mentioned in Nagarjunakonda inscriptions. The royal ladies were challenging men in literary and religious discourses. Even ordinary women were not all illiterate. They could write letters to their husbands in distant lands, according to Gathasaptasati even in Satavahana age. The trend would have continued in the Ikshavaku period. Vesyas or prostitutes well versed in fine arts, especially of music and dance could overcome their degraded position in society by mingling with the higher classes because of their accomplishments.

Not much is known about women in Andhradesa during the period of the four centuries from mid 3rd Century when Ikshavaku rule declined till mid 7th Century AD when the entire country came under the sway of the Chalukyas of Vengi. Avanitalantavati, the Princess of the Anandagotras of the Krishna Valley and the queen of Madhavavarma of the Vishnukundins and a princess of the Vakataka Kingdom were remembered for their participation in religious rites and charities. The peak period of Buddhism had declined and the first Hindu temple was that of Chitraradhasvami at Pedavegi near Ellore (end of the 3rd or beginning of the 4th century AD) enjoying the patronage of the Salankayanas. The trend of building temples was continued by the Vishnukundins *e.g.* Mogalrajapuram caves. Women made substantial gifts to temples and occasionally to Buddhist shrines. Though unrecorded, substantial advancement leading to the elevation of women in this period must have taken place.

THE EASTERN CHALUKYA EMPIRE (AD 624-1075)

Women in the Empire of the Chalukyas of Vangi had fared better than in the preceding three centuries in their different roles as wives, mothers, religious benefactors, scholars and landladies. The Chalukyas, the political successors of the Salankayanas, by a series of conquests established and consolidated their kingdom embracing the entire Andhradesa. With tranquility, peace and prosperity prevalent in the country, women could concentrate and indulge themselves in nation-building activities which mirror their aspirations.

(*a*) *Royal ladies and diplomatic matrimonial alliances*—Royal mothers, queens and princesses figure in the several long inscriptions serving as the sources for the growth of Sanskrit and Telugu language and literature, relegating Prakrit to the background. *e.g.* Ayyanamahadevi was the queen of Kubjavishnuvardhana (AD 624-641), the brother of Pulakesin II and founder of the dynasty. Vijayamahadevi was the queen of Vishnuvardhana III (AD 719-755). Silamahadevi, the daughter of King Dhruva of the Rashtrakutas was the pattamahishi of Vishnuvardhana IV (AD 772-808), a testimony to inter-state matrimonial alliances. Another Silamahadevi alias Bhattarika was the queen of Vishnuvardhana V (AD 847-849) was the daughter of Kakka Suvarnavarsha of Ghurjaradesa. A third Silamahadevi, the daughter of Indravallabha, the younger brother of Govinda III of the Rashtrakutas was the mother of Gunagavijayditya (AD 849-892), the greatest ruler of the Chalukyas. Among the three queens of King Bhima II (AD 934-945), Lokamba hails from the Eastern Ganga dynasty of Kalinga.

More powerful than these alliances were the alliances of the Chalukyas with the Imperial Cholas. Vimaladitya's (AD 1011-1018) queen Kundavai or Kunda Mahadevi was the daughter of Rajaraja, the Great. It is another queen Melamba the daughter of Jatachoda. Ammangadevi, the daughter of Rajendra I Chola was the queen of Rajaraja Narendra (AD 1019-1061), her cousin and son of Vimaladitya. Rajendra Kulottunga, their son became the founder of the Chalukya Chola Empire. Madhavadevi of Haihaya lineage and Revaladevi were the queens of Vijayaditaya II (AD 1062-1073). Princess Somaladevi was the daughter of Revaladevi.

(*b*) *Religion*—The entire range of huge religious edifices and monuments in the Coastal Andhradesa, especially from Simhachalam to Srikakulam near Machilipatnam was the work of the Eastern Chalukya rulers signifying their military conquests, consequent gratitude to deities and desiring further benefits and religious merit for their ancestors, themselves and their progeny. Women of all cadres from the royal to the lay layers by their enthusiasm, instigation, bold initiative and multifarious activities were the motive force in building these temples. Of the few Jaina tamples of the period, the one at Vijayawada was built by Queen Ayyana Mahadevi.

Buddhism decayed rapidly and all Buddhist stupas of the Satavahanas and the Ikshvakus were converted into Hindu temples of Siva and Vishnu and developed into huge temple complexes *e.g.* Chebrole, Pithapur, Bezwada. The 108 Narendresvara temples were built by Vijayaditya II after his earlier name Narendresvara to commemorate his 108 victories in battles in a period of twelve years. Chalukya Bhima I built the Bimesvara temples at Draksharama and Chalukya Bhimavanram after his name. These together with the temples of Kshirarama (Palakol), Somarama (Gunupudi) and Amaravati, constructed in this period became celebrated as the Pancharamas and Panchatirthas, indicating their genesis to Buddhism. They continue to this day as the most important among the centres of pilgrimage in Andhradesa. Almost evergy village in Andhradesa has a temple in the Chalukyan style of architecture.

Inscriptions attest to the large gifts of pillars, land, animals, lamps and paraphernalia for the maintenance of temples by ladies. Provision for perpetual lamps was most popular donation with women of all classes. Could it have ever been possible for the building of temples, their maintenance and the institution of festivals without the full cooperation of women? On the other hand, women would have influenced men when they were receptive and some women when they had no response from men could implement their own desires with the help of women of similar temperament and disposition and succeed in their efforts.

MEDIEVAL PERIOD

In this period, the frequent Muslim invasions and the resultant apprehension of pollution and contamination, a severe blow to prevalent Varnasramadharama, led to several stresses and afflictions which women of all classes had to confront. These were in the form of seclusion, veil or purdah, early marriages, sahagamana or sati, polygamy, lack of free movement in political, in administrative, religious, economic and literary spheres besides, a host of other inhibitions. But history shows how these several obstacles and hurdles were overcome by women and their consequent advancement and elevation. The laurels were won by women by capacities, capabilities, struggle and fight and not received as gifts by contemporary society.

The Kakatiya Empire (*AD 1000-1323*)—In the three centuries of the Kakatiya rule, Andhradesa reached unscaled heights in its multifaceted development in expansion—political and economic—particularly in commerce, administration, religion, literature and fine arts. The huge temples and irrigation tanks in the three regions—Telangana, Coastal Andhra and Rayalasima, still remain as the glowing tribute to the beneficial Kakatiya rule. The several subsidiary dynasties had a major share in meeting the challenges within the Empire and outside from the Muslim invaders and rulers of other Kingdoms.

(*a*) *Matrimonial alliances*—Diplomatic marriage alliances with contemporary royal families and powerful subsidiary ruling families and feudatories attesting to the power of women to influence boldly their partners in life were on the increase in this period *e.g.* Princess Padmakshi, the queen of Rudradeva Maharaja I (AD 1158-1195) was the daughter of Buddhadeva of the Gona Haihayas of Vardhamanapura. Kakatiya princesses Kundambika and Mailama, the daughters of King Mahadeva (AD 1195-1198) were married to Rudra, the ruler Netavadi kingdom. Their brother Ganapati (AD 1199-1259) had a long reign of sixty years, a most fruitful period in Andhra history. Naramba and Peramba, the daughters of Pinachoda of Ayya lineage of Divisima and sisters of Jayapasenani were the queens of Ganapatideva. Rudrama and Ganapama, the daughters of Ganapati, married prince Virabhadra of the Chalukyas of Nidadavole and Keta of the Kota kingdom respectively. Meiama, the sister of Ganapati was married to Rudra of the Natavadis. These several ladies had a powerful double edged impact on the kingdoms from which they hailed and the kingdoms which they entered.

(*b*) *Political personalities*—In the 13th Century, when the country was hot prepared to tolerate woman as its ruler, Rudrama (AD 1259-1295) and Ganapama, the two sisters and daughters of King Ganapati could rule in Andhradesa, overcoming the challenges of sex and afflictions of political, religious and economic nature.

(1) *Rudrama*: From childhood, Rudrama was trained as a boy by Ganpatideva in the arts of war and administration to succeed him on the throne. She was known as Rudradeva Maharaja and attended royal duties in masculine robes. She fought battles in military attire riding a horse with sword in hand. From three years prior to her father's death, Rudrama was associated with the administration of the Empire—central and provincial. She was the first lady ruler in South India as Sultana Razia Begum was in Northern India.

Rudrama had to face the challenges of the jealousy and wrath of rulers of neighbouring kingdoms and internal rebellions. But she could overcome these hurdles in the initial stages and subsequent years of her rule and bestow on her people the benefits of tranquility, peace and prosperity. For example, when in her absence, her two illegitimate brothers, the sons of Ganapati occupied the throne, she killed them and enthroned herself and the nobles who helped in this peril, proudly assumed the title of Kakatiyarajyasthapanacharya. She successfully beat back the invasion of Yadava Mahadeva (AD 1268) on Warangal and chased him upto Devagiri. But Yadava inscriptions speak of the invasion as a victory and satirically say that knowing that he would not kill a woman, the Telugu people saved themselves by having Rudrama on the throne. In her conquests and consolidation and administration, Rudrama had full loyal support of the ministers—mahapradhanis and mahasenapatis hailing from the Induluri and Viriyala and Gona families *e.g.* Induluri Annayadeva and Viriyala Kamasani.

Rudrama repaired the strong fortress at Warangal *i.e.* Ekasilanagara and rendered it impregnable. The two grades of army were the royal army and the feudal army and the four kinds of forts were hill forts *e.g.* Hanumakonda, forest forts *e.g.* Kanduru, water forts *e.g.* Divi and Kolanu and plain forts *e.g.* Orugallu. Administration by officers *e.g.* Niyogis, Adyakshas was efficient. Several tanks called samudrams and canals were dug all over the kingdom for irrigation. Agriculture was in good condition due to the services of the noble Malyala and Recharla families.

Several mathas and temples were built in Rudrama's reign. The Golakimatha established at Mandara village was for the propagation of Saivism. A choultry (annasatra), hospital for children and adults were added to the matha by guru Visvesvarasambhu. The flourishing state of industries trade and commerce and maritime activities in Rudrama's kingdom were attested by Marco Polo, the Venetian traveller who visited Motupalle and praised the excellent rule of the queen.

Rudrama had taken after her father in progeny and had two daughters Mummadamma and Ruyyamma and married them to Mahadevaraju of the Chalukyas and Induluri Annayya respectively. She adopted Prataparudra, the son of Mummadamma and decided that he should succeed her on the throne as she succeeded Ganapati. She must have considered selecting one of her daughters or both daughters jointly as her successors but her experience may have made her think that a man would be better fitted to face the oncoming onslaughts of the Muslims which she did not experience. It was not to be so; and even Prataparudra could not save the kingdom.

(2) *Ganapama*: The younger sister of Rudrama, Ganapama Devi distinguished herself as joint ruler with her husband Kota Beta LL for 20 years and on his premature demise as the sole sovereign of the Kota Kingdom comprising Velanadu 6000 country *i.e.* Shatsahasravani for a long period of forty years. Trained as warrior and administrator like Rudramadevi, Ganapama assumed the title of Maharaja and protected the kingdom for sixty years with devotion in the welfare of her subjects. She donated lavishly for the maintenance of temples, mathas and tanks for irrigation.

(3) *Aravilli Nagamma*: Celebrated in history as Nayakuralu, this lady could sway the Haihaya Kingdom of Palnad challenging with tremendous success the diplomacy and manouvres of Brahmanayadu, the most powerful and hereditary minister of the Haihayas with capital at Gurijala. Daughter of Jagga Reddi and wife of a Patna Reddi, Nagamma overcoming the conventional seclusion of women developed into an outstanding warrior and eminent administrator. The methods she followed to reach this position in the state attests to her sagacity. One day, while King Anuguraja was returning from a hunting expedition, Nagamma invited him to her village and treated him and his retinue to such immense satisfaction that the king asked her to express her desire. Nagamma revealed her desire to be the minister of his kingdom for 7 ghadiyas when she wished and secured from him an order to that effect with the royal seal affixed on it. From that time she was making frequent visits to the court and felt that she was treated with honour by

one and all except Brahmanayadu. Just waiting to pay Brahmanayadu in his own coin, Nagamma by showing the order of Anuguraja to his successor Nalagamaraja on the death of the former became his minister. By creating differences between Nalagama and Brahmanayadu Nalagama and his brothers Mallideva etc., she succeeded in dividing the kingdom. Her diplomacy gradually led to the war of Palnad and ultimate destruction of the kingdom. She fought so valiantly taking a toll of many warriors though finally she was destined to suffer defeat and extinction at the hands of Brahmanayadu. Nagamma's role reveals how far a woman could go in protecting her honour by her stratagem, capacities and valour when challenged by men. For her drive and boldness and qualities of leadership, she was known as Nayakuralu *i.e.* lady leader.

(4) *Silama*: This lady, the mother of Brahmanayadu, the arch rival of Nagamma in politics, was well versed in polity, religious and social lore of the period. She could recognise the movements of spies in the absence of her son. She was helping Brahmanayadu in administering the kingdom, as the royal mothers of the Satavahana and Ikshvaku periods. When going to the battlefield, Silama advised her son that tribals, shepherds, fuelmen and men sheltering in temples and hiding behind wives should be spared. That was contemporary political wisdom. Perhaps that is the reason at present for temples being used as arsenals *e.g.* Golden Temple at Amritsar.

(c) *Religion and Society*—Though Islam was responsible for the afflictions of seclusion, early marriages, purdah, sahagamana of women, the impact of Virasaivism and Vaishnavism was profound on society in Andhradesa. These vigorous religions, with ideals to counter and attack Islamic onslaughts with sword in hand brought about a revolution in contemporary Andhradesa. The propagators of Virasaivism namely Basaveswara and Mallikarjuna Pandita preached that women should have equal rights with men and could disobey men in certain matters and at certain times *e.g.* a wife should teach her husband to become a devotee of Siva if he was not so and in case he does not obey her, she should divorce him says Sivatatvasara. Virasaivism propagated the abrogation of caste distinctions.

Women of higher classes had the right to spend lavishly in building temples, mathas and choultries and provide for their maintenance *e.g.* in AD 1208 Erakasanamma of Pillalamarri noble family installed Erakasamudram, a matha called Erukamatha in it and a choultry and gave lands for maintenance. She arranged for Calivendru to provide butter milk to wayfarers.

Dancing girls had a respectable status in society. Living with kings, nobles and in service of temples, these women were not married but remained in contact with one man just like married ladies and remained single on his decease. Such bhogastris are mentioned as 'Lanjapendlamu' in inscriptions and common parlance. The dancing girls were specially trained in music and dance. They were dancers and musicians in royal courts and temples. By their expertise in arts, they were held in high esteem in society, some times on par with queens in royal families.

Besides the Bhogastries, the sanis also called Devadasis were the dancing girls in the service of temples. Experts in music, dance and fine arts, the sanis dedicated their lives to the service of god. In case they married, they lost their profession of serving in temples. From childhood, the sanis were trained in fine arts and Sanskrit and vernacular languages by a dance master. The period of their training was from the fifth year till the fourteenth year. The girls then had to take an examination in the temple compound. If successful, they were appointed as sanis or Devadasis in the service of god. If they failed in the test, they were considered as prostitutes in society. The tradition that Devadasis had divine origin and therefore competent to serve deities attests to their powerful position in medieval society. Machala Devi was an adept dancer in the court of Prataparudra of Warangal.

Not merely Bhogastris and sanis or Devadasis but there were also the Vesyas who indulged in immoral trafic by attracking rich men by evil devices and rendered them paupers. Living in separate quarters known as vesyavatikas or sanivadas, these women were classified into fifty categories dependent on their nature, character and beauty etc. Thus women by means of vices could challenge and succeed in overcoming men of luxury and of licentious character.

Tribal women were leading independent lives. Among them, the women of Eruka tribe were experts in predicting future of a person by studying the palm. They predicted in the particular tune of a song popularly known as Sodhe with oft repetition in it. Living in jungles, the Eruka women had easy entry into royal palaces, noble mansions forecasting victories in campaigns, meeting of their lovers etc. Nomadic, going from place to place, the Eruka women and not men had the power of prediction and thus had a status in contemporary society. The women of the Sabara tribe, not nomadic like the Erukas, but settled in jungles had equal rights with their husbands and were never subservient to them. Not merely that they could discharge household duties, they were bold and courageous and could handle with dexterity bows and arrows and hunt animals. The Sabara women could study the animals thoroughly—their nature and appearance. Thus the tribal women had unique power of prophecy and valour.

(*d*) *Education and Literature*—While higher education was accessible to women of higher classes, women of lower classes, could acquire knowledge in purans, puranic lore, the stories of Ramayana, Mahabharata and Bhagavata by attending and listening to discourses in temples daily and during festivals. For example, during Sivaratri festival especially in Srisailam, women used to vie with men in listening to the stories of Siva says Palkuriki Somanatha in his Panditha-aradhya Charitra. They used to keep awake throughout the nightsinging songs in praise of Siva.

There were lady poetesses who by their grit, valour and boldness were prepared to sacrifice their lives and those of their husbands for prestige for posterity. Poetess Chanamamba was the devoted wife of Khadgatikkana, celebrated as Ranatikkana and sister-in-law of Kavibrahma Tikkana Somayaji. The two Tikkanas were in the court of King Manumasiddhi III of the Telugu Chodas of Nellore. The mother of Khadgatikkana was also a poetess like his wife. Tradition has it that once when Khadgatikkana fled from the battlefield and returned home, both his mother and wife derided him by comparing him with themselves and with defeated cattle and spilt milk so vigorously in Telugu verses that he immediately went back to the battlefield and vanquished his enemies. Such was the nonchalant and determined attitude of women of the age regarding prestige. The verses are fine literary pieces in Telugu literature.

THE REDDI, THE VELAMA AND THE VIJAYANAGAR KINGDOMS

The Kingdoms of the Reddis of Kondavidu and Rajahmundry (AD 1320-1448), the Velamas of Rachakonda and Devarakonda and the Empire of Vijayanagar (AD 1336-1665) were contemporaneous and ever engaged in conflicts and alliances for territorial expansion and suzerainty.

(*a*) *Matrimonial alliances*—Princess Doddamba and her sister, the daughters of Prolayavema Reddi (AD 1325-53) the founder of the Reddi Kingdom were married to Immadi Kataya Reddi, a noble and Bhimalinga Choda of the Telugu Chodas of Rajahmundry as a political diplomatic measure to strengthen the Kingdom. In continuation of this policy, Doddamba, the daughter of King Anavota Reddi (ADI 1353-64) became the queen of Kataya Vema Reddi, the King's nephew. Princesses Anitalli and Hariharamba, the two daughters of Kataya Vema Reddi (AD 1395-1414), the founder of the Rajahmundry Reddi Kingdom were married to Virabhadra Reddi and Vema Reddi respectively. The brothers were the two sons of Allada Reddi, a powerful noble in the Kingdom. No doubt these ladies of the royal family were adept in warfare and administration.

(*b*) *Administrators*—Queen Anitalli, the daughter of Kataya Vema succeeded him on the throne at Rajahmundry and ruled jointly with her husband Virabhadra Reddi. The joint rule was a measure to strengthen the administration against foreign or

Muslim incursions. Well versed in the arts of war and peace, Anitalli was an efficient ruler in contemporary Andhradesa and issued grants in her own name.

(*c*) *Religion and Society*—As in the previous ages, women in the Reddi age indulged in religious activities as building of temples, auxiliaries in temples and making rich gifts to Gods ranging from lamps to lands desiring perpetual merit to their ancestors, themselves and their progeny e.g. princesses, queens. Huge tanks and irrigational canals were constructed. For example, Queen Suraima Devi, the queen of Peda Komati Vema dug a huge tank called Santkana Sagara at the Capital Kondavidu and her son Prince Racha Vema constructed a feeder canal to it called Jaganobbaganda Kalava, after a title in the Reddi prasasti.

(*d*) *Fine Arts*—Dance and music flourished under the patronage of the Reddi Kings. The annual Vasantotsavas or spring festivals were unique features of the age besides the temple festivals. They were the occasions for the exuberance of jubilant and happy mingling of all classes of people and performances of dance and music. The Devadasis and court dancers had a large role in the spring festivals. For example Lakuma Devi, the preyasi of King Kumaragiri Reddi was a celebrated dancer attested by inscriptions and contemporary literary work Vasantarajiya, a commentary on Kumaragirirajiya, a work on dramaturgy. She made rich gifts to temples.

Vijayanagar Empire—Andhradesa was partially an integral poet of the Empire of Vijayanagar. According to Nicolo de Corti, women were riding on horses while accompanying the King. Courtesan was the last of the twelve queens of the King, says Paes. Each queen had a separate mansion and it was totally administered by women. The queens were extremely rich. Among the women employed in the palace, some were trained in fighting with sword, some were wrestlers and there were also beaters of drums, gardeners and soldiers. The legend of Mallisvari who refused the hand of a king and thereby incurred his displeasure leading to war illustrates the independent nature of rural women and their courage and boldness even to sacrifice their lives for their liberty. They were prepared to face any challenge.

Fine Arts and Literature—In Andhradesa and during the Nayak rule at Tanjore and Madurai there flourished women who were famous dancers and musicians and scholars and poetesses. They were Tallapaka Timmakka, Atukuri Molla, Mohanangi, Tukkadevi, Tirumalamba, Ramabhadramba, Madhuravani, Krishnajamma, Rangajamma and Muddupalani. They were learned in Sanskrit and Telugu languages.

Among these, Molla was the first woman to has written Ramayana in Telugu verse. Tirmulamba was the author of Varadambikaparinayamu *i.e.* the marriage of Varadambika with Achutaraya. Ramabhadramba was the author of Raghunatha-bhyudaya i.e. king Raghunatha of Tanjore. Gangadevi was the author of Mathuravijayamu. Tradition has it that Maduravani who could write poetry of four varieties vanquished in literary discourses the scholars of Saraswati Bhavan at Madura and shifted it to Tanjore. Muddupalani's great Prabhanda is Radhikasanth vivahamu with intense erotic theme. So there were women who could challenge successfully men in literature in this period.

MODERN PERIOD

Andhradesa was under Kutbshahis and Asafjahis of Nizam in the early part of the modern age—the 17th and 18th centuries and lay prostrate at the feet of the British by the dawn of the 19th century. The caste system, untouchability and the heinous condition of women—especially the prevalence of Sati, female infanticide, the veil, the dowry, child marriages, prostitution and lack of education became deep rooted because of the impact of Muslim rule. Consequent on the work of a series of social reformers, socio-religious reform associations and government legislation in the 19th century and political agitation for independence in the 20th century in its various phases an awareness, an awakening was created among women. The women slowly and steadily emerged from their positions of seclusion and shelter, challenging the severe social and religious inhibitions, their innate capacities flowed out and they distinguished themselves in the movements of revival and renaissance and most enchanting, the freedom struggle under Mahatma Gandhi. After Independence, there is total improvement in their position in every sphere almost on equal par with men. But still so much remains to be done to eradicate illiteracy, poverty and establish literacy, prosperity, happiness and welfare.

(*a*) *Sati or Sahagamana*—There are instances of self immolation *i.e.* a wife burning herself on the funeral pyre of her husband in the 12th and 13th centuries in Andhradesa. This custom continued in the Vijayanagar Empire. A series of government Acts in 1812, 1815 and 1817 prevented Sati in certain cases—very young women, pregnant women and women with infants. But finally, the Act of 1829 by Lord William Bentinck, with the support of Raja Ram Mohan Roy completely abolished this evil social custom. This came to the rescue of many women who were forced to die as Sati promising them external fame, immortality and heaven. Mostly confined to royal and affluent families, Sati was not common in Andhradesa.

(*b*) *Child marriages*—Child marriages to secure girl's protection and giving of dowries for the maintenance of the child wife by the bridegroom and his parents were the evils widely prevalent in the colonial period in Andhradesa. After paying huge dowries, some families were ruined due to bankruptcy. The daughters of parents who could not afford to give huge amounts as dowry became the victims of their poverty as they were married to elderly men in second marriage or even third marriage with wide difference of age ranging from fifteen to even fifty years. The parents of the girls used to receive bride's price *i.e.* kanyasulkam. As such girls were married prior to the attainment of age to avoid social boycott, they had hardly learnt the three Rs and after marriage they were immersed in household duties and so opportunities to become literate were remote even if they desired. That desire was rare due to suppression and oppression. So from childhood, women had to develop blind belief in doing whatever they were asked to do by men. For want of literacy, they could not verify the good from the evil or bad from the worse.

THE MOVEMENT FOR WOMEN'S UPLIFT

Taking advantage of the English education, some of the social and religious reformers enlightened by the progress of women in Europe realised that if the housewife is educated, the children's future would be brighter. So they launched a multi-faceted movement for the fulfledged development and upliftment of women. The diflerent phases of the movement were (a) widow remarriage (b) women's education (c) postpuberty marriages (d) abolition of prostitution and (e) literary revivalism.

(*a*) *Remarriage*—Remarriage movement in Andhradesa was led by Kandukuri Viresalingam and was continued by Venkataratnam Naidu, Ramakrishna Rao and others. It had its beginnings in the writings of Samineni Muddu Narasimha Nayanivaru, a social reformer, in his Journal Hitasuchani. Highlighting the sufferings of the widow, he exhorted wisemen to eradicate such longstanding sinister customs in society. Viresalingam in his Journal Vivekavardhani and the volume of lecturers, kindled in the minds of men a change by emphasising the evils of compulsory widowhood and propagated remarriage citing the approval of such a step in the Smritis.

Having prepared the ground by writings and speeches, Viresalingam launched on the sacred task of performing remarriage of young widows Viresalingam Pantulu, the champion of the movement, proved that early marriages had no sanction in the Sastras. The evil of bride's price paid by the widowers to the parents of the girls were motivated by the belief that a man dying when wife is alive would reach heaven and parents by getting their girls married would acquire religious merit.

The first step to eradicate child marriage was to give education to girls. Slowly girls from some familes could go in for higher education and even employment. Middle class families could realise the merits of post-puberty marriages, as their girls could have better health, facilities for education and concurrent depreciation of bride's price and even dowry. For some time the families with their girls attaining age prior to marriage had to face strict social ostracism—none would visit them, dine with them etc. Even for those girls to be married after puberty, to find bridegrooms was difficult as in the case of remarriages and very few persons would attend the marriages. Even to get priests to conduct marriages was a problem. But the reformers were undaunted by these. hurdles. Gradually the movement became widespread and Government legislation—The Age of Consent Act of 1929—gave legal protection to the work of the social reformers. In rural areas, the early marriages continue to take place but post-puberty marriages are most common and popular.

(*b*) *Abolition of prostitution*—The traditional profession of prostitution, a blot on Hindu society came into disrepute by the preachings and work of Viresalingam and his followers in Andhradesa. To the orthodox section of society arguing that the arts of music and dance would die if prostitution is eradicated, Viresalingam proclaimed 'so long these fine arts continue to remain the property of the dancing girls, family or caste girls will not like to learn them feeling that it is below their prestige to learn them.' Emphasising that from early times dance and music were learnt by women of all classes and not confined to prostitutes, he addressed prostitutes to give up their heinous profession and lead their lives like women in other classes of society. The impact of the work of the social reformers with the help of the reform movements particularly Brahmo is clear in that gradually the dancing parties *e.g.* Bhogam melams during marriages and marriage processions, very common and popular, had declined and had ceased to exist. Gurujada Appa Rao, a contemporary powerful writer aiming at elevation of condition of women in his celebrated drama Kanyasulkam describes the evil intentions of the prostitutes, the hardships of men who were attracted by them, the difficulties of destitute child widows, the nautch parties and the merits of remarriage. The easily accessible from 1881 onwards. In that year, Venkataratnam Naidu, a disciple of Mannava Butchayya Pantulu of Madras, a Brahmosamajist, celebıated two remarriages at Rajahmundry. Viresalingam successfully carried on his work, in the beginning with the help of Brahmosamaj Movement quite vigorous in Andhradesa. He established Widow's Homes at Rajahmundry and Madras. Viresalingam and his family and disciples and followers had to suffer severe social ostracism for their remarriage activities. The newly married couples also had to face hardships of social boycott. But these challenges were met by them with the full and wholehearted support of their benefactors, Viresalingam and his wife Rajyalaksmi who gave complete cooperation to her husband in his reform activities. Remarriage movement continued vigorously so long as Viresalingam lived and was entrusted by him on his death bed (1917) to his disciples especially Dr. Laksmipathi. Subsequently it merged with the political movement of Freedom Srruggle with the emergence of Gandhi on the political arena. For this great service of Viresalingam Andhradesa was hailed as 'Viresalingam's Andhra'.

(*c*) *Women's Education*—The first separate school for girls was started by the social reformer, Mannava Butchayyapantulu in Madras. "Unless women's position is improved and housewives are educated leading to wisdom, our country will not prosper" proclaimed Viresalingam Pantulu. He not only propagated but also established schools for girls at Rajahmundry. As girls after attaining age were reluctant to go to schools with men teachers, he appointed women teachers in those schools. He provided to run adult education centres in the evenings for the education of housewives. The Hitakarini Samaj School, a co-educational institution, was the work of Viresalingam to provide opportunities to boys and girls to come together to inculcate mutual regard. Gradually several schools for girls in all important towns in Andhradesa were started by the reformers, the Christian missions and the Government *e.g.* Masulipatnam, Kakinada, Rajahmundry, Visakhapatnam. Women's education in Kakinada progressed due to the activities of Venkataratnam Naidu. There were orphanages for women at Rajahmundry and Kakinada.

(*d*) *Post puberty marriages*—The inculcation, propagation and expansion of the movement for the performance of post-puberty marriages was to meet the challenge of the widespread evil of child marriages, more common among higher castes. The marriages of girls between the ages of three and ten leading to compulsory widowhood, lack of education and premature motherhood leading to physical weakness, premature old age and premature death; weak children vulnerable to diseases. Presiding in her court encouraged women to participate in public academic discussions, deliver lectures and propagate ideals of reform among masses. Kandukuri Rajyalakshmamma, a devotee, composed songs of prayer to Ekesvara, built a Prarthana mandira at Rajahmundry, the first Prarthana Samaj exclusively for women in Andhradesa. She dared helping Harijans and orphans challenging orthodoxy. Rani Sankaramma of Vanaparti, Gadwala Adilakshmamma and Ravichettu Lakshminarasamma were also prominent literary women of the age. Some of the women journalists were Balantrapu Seshamamba, the editor of 'Hindusundari', Vinjamuri Venkataratnamma, the editor of 'Anasuya' and Pulugurti Laksminarasamamba, the editor of 'Savitri.' These eminent leaders, challenging contemporary journals edited by men, devoted their services to expose the problems of women and fight for their elevation through the media of journalism.

FREEDOM STRUGGLE

Braving all the challenges—social, religious and economic—Andhra women with the awakening resulting from the Reform Movement jumped into the political movement for liberation of India from colonialism. Their role was effective, remarkable and memorable and won the praise of Mahatma Gandhi. With courage, confidence, determination and boldness, women in Andhradesa of rank and file distinguished themselves in contributing their mite and sacrificing everything, sometimes their lives as well, in participating in the multifaceted freedom struggle for the attainment of Swaraj for Bharat or Indian Independence (1947).

(*a*) *Non-Cooperation Movement*—Prior to the emergence of Mahatma Gandhi to political arena, women were not active in the political struggle. When Mahatma Gandhi rendered the Satyagraha or Non-violent Movement a mass movement in which men and women, the rich and the poor, the higher caste people and untouchables, rural and urban, educated and the illiterate could have free entry, women irrespective of caste, class and religion, releasing themselves from the shackles of home life, participated in this political adventure with great enthusiasm. Mahatma Gandhi exhorted women to come forward and play a major role and the response of the women made the movement a tremendous success. The women boldly sustained lathi blows, courted imprisonment and spent years in rigorous imprisonment. The first Andhra lady who responded to the call of the Mahatma in 1920 was Duvvuri Subbamma. A child widow wearing a veil, learned and of a philosophical bent of mind, she could lecture to huge audiences of five to six thousand people when there were no mikes. She received lathi blows several times and courted imprisonment on many occasions. From Ellore, Kalagara Pichchamma was the leader of the chance or possibility of child widows not remarried to take to prostitution, the author explained in Kanyasulkam. By means of Harikatha Kalakshepams from Ramayana, Mahabharata, the lives of saints, heroes from history, the social reformers could wean away masses of prostitutes, widows and unfortunate sections of society from their notorious professions and mistaken aptitudes and encourage them to take to good professions and family lives *e.g.* Kauta Srirama Sastri and Cherukuvada Venkatanarasimham at Machilipatnam and other towns in Andhradesa; Adipudi Somanatha Rao at Madras and in Andhradesa. Finally by the Devadasi Abolition Act sponsored by Dr. Muthulakshmi Reddi, the role of dancing girls in temples and processions of God had its exit.

(*b*) *Literary Revival*—In the middle of the 19th century, Tarigonda Venkamamba, a child widow and a devotee of Lord Venkatachalapathi of Tirumala, unable to bear the social hindrances, left her parents and home at Tarigonda (Cudappah District) and settled in Tirupati. She wrote every variety of songs on the God and eleven literary works—all with puranic themes. She wrote in couplet metre, Yakshagana, Sataka, kavya, nataka and prabandha styles. She was the first Andhra poetess to have written such a variety of compositions. The period of half a century consisting of the last quarter of the 19th century and the first quarter of the 20th century, constituted the age of social reform synonymous with the age of Viresalingam for his total involvement and sacrifice in the upliftment of women crowned with tremendous success. The Government recognised his services by conferring the title of Rao Bahadur. Viresalingam was the Father of modern Andhra as he was the pioneer in the creation of modern Telugu language and literature *i.e.* novel, short story, drama, prose, parody, biography, autobiography, travels, tales, science journalism etc. every variety prevalent in English language. Several women who benefited by the educational facilities distinguished themselves as writers, journalists, teachers, educationists, founders and secretaries of women's associations, and protagonists of reform. Some of them were Kottkalpudi Sitamma, a disciple of Viresalingam and a teacher in the royal family of Pithapur, Kamarajugadda Sundaramme and Sugunamahalakshmamma' teachers at Rajahmundry, Bhandaru Acchamamba, the sister of Komarraju Lakshmana Rao, an eminent historian and Rani Chinnamamba, the Maharani of Pithapur. While Sitamma rendered Ramayana in Telugu prose, Achchamamba's magnum opus was Abalasachcharitramala—the history of women, in three parts devoted to women of Puranic age, historical period and women of foreign lands. Rani Chinnamamba by arranging literary discourses and scholars' meets exclusively of women and herself movement. Her daughter, Maganti Annapurnadevi, ready to go to America in 1920 for higher studies, stayed back to participate in the Movement and became an endeared follower of Mahatma Gandhi. Some of the well known ladies were

Jayanti Suramma of Vizianagaram, Tallapragada Visvasundaramma of Rajahmundry, Devulapalli Satyavatamma of Tanuku, Unnava Lakshmibayamma and Konda Parvatidevi of Guntur, Bharatidevi Ranga of Nidubrolu and Manapaka Kamalamma and Dronamraju Lakshmibayamma of Machilipatnam.

(c) *Council Entry and Constructive Programme*—In the decade from the Non-Cooperation Movement till the launching of the Salt Satyagraha or Civil Disobedience Movement, women's participation in every phase of the freedom struggle—foreign boycott, Swadeshi and Khaddar and prohibition—had increased by leaps and bounds. They had full support of men as entire families became involved in the movement. Bonfires of huge piles of foreign cloth was a common sight in every road in towns and villages and women took to Khaddar and picketing of liquor shops and eradication of untouchability. Almost every house possessed as many charkas or spinning wheels as the members of the family to intensify the production of yarn. Some women engaged themselves in the more difficult avocation of weaving in leisure hours. Some of the prominent women of this period were Manapragada Ramasundaramma from Telingana who joined the Movement in 1926 at the age of twelve. She represented the area in the conference of women leaders of Andhra Province at Guntur (1933) and was jailed for this activity and lost her life in a year due to ill health. Chunduru Ratnamma, a Zamindar of Vaisya community in Ellore came out of seclusion and participated in public meetings. She was a member of Congress Working Committee of Ellore for many years. Vedantam Kamaladevi was the chief of women volunteers' corps at the Congress session at Kakinada (1924). Unnava Lakshmibayamma of Guntur established a Girls' School—Saradaniketanam—in 1922. Since 1908 she was running an orphanage and Widows' Home in Guntur. In Nellore, Ponaka Kanakamma of Reddi community, a disciple of Gandhi, founded Kasturibai Gandhi Girl's School. She, in conjunction with Dronamaraju Lakshmibayamma, translated Gita into beautiful Telugu. Kanchanapalli Kanakamma was a well known poetess of this age. Achanta Rukminamma of Madras was the Secretary of the Madras Branch of All India Women's Association and started Swadeshi Stores totall managed by women. She had a large role in the constructive programme and represented India in the International Women's Suffrage Alliance Congress at Paris (1926). On return, she became a member of District Board, Chingleput and Corporation of Madras.

(*d*) *Civil Disobedience Movement*—Enthralled by the clarion call of Mahatma Gandhi to entire humanity in India to jump into the Salt Satyagraha Movement, (1930) women and children whole heartedly met the challenge by complete self sacrifice and total obedience to his command. While the ladies already engaged in constructive programme joined this Civil Disobedience Movement courted prison repeatedly and sometimes with fatal consequences, the mass of women swelled the movement and made it a tremendous success. Old women, pregnant women participated in the Satyagraha and underwent rigorous imprisonment. Women political prisoners had to cook for hundreds of prisoners, husk large quantities of paddy and carry heavy loads. They had to sleep on the bare floor and live for several days on mere kanji. Many children born in jails were given the names of Krishna and Maya *e.g.* Tekumalla Varahalamma had her child Maya in the prison at Vizianagaram. When leaders were in prison, women took over and led the movement *e.g.* Unnava Lakshmibayamma in Guntur and Durgabai Deshmukh in Madras.

(*e*) *Congress in power*—When Congress Ministry was formed in Madras in 1937 with C. Rajagopalachari as Premier, Mrs. Rukmini Lakshmipati became the Deputy Speaker of the Civil Disobedience Movement.

(*f*) *Quit India Movement & Individual Satyagraha Movement*—Women, both in numbers and worth, made remarkable contribution by their sacrifices and dedication for the success of these phases of the Freedom struggle headed by Mahatma Gandhi *e.g.* Rukmini Lakshmipati.

(*g*) *Congress in power* (*1946*)—In the Congress Ministry with Andhrakesari T. Prakasam as Premier, Mrs. Rakmini Lakshmipati was the Minister for Health. She was responsible for the establishment of Medical College at Guntur and upgrading of the Indian School of Medicine, Madras into a college.

INDIAN INDEPENDENCE & FORMATION OF ANDHRA PRADESH

With the achievement of Indian Independence and formation of Andhra Pradesh after tremendous sacrifices by the people, outlets for progress of women had multiplied. They are eligible for open competition in every profession—public and private. There are eminent women writers, historians, musicians, dancers, sportswomen, film stars, film directors as also Judges, Ministers and Administrators. But all this development is still considerably away from the women and children in the rural areas steeped in ignorance and poverty. Unless they are rescued from these vices, there is no happiness, prosperity and culture in entire Andhra Pradesh. Still women have to meet the challenge steadfastly and achieve victory.

BIBLIOGRAPHY

Sircar: Select Inscriptions Volume I

K. Gopalachari: Early History of Andhra Country (1941), Madras

A. Rea: South Indian Buddhist Antiquities, Vol. VI (1894) Epigraphica Indica, Vol. VIII

The Indian Academy of Art, Vol. 21, Calcutta

M. Rama Rao: Satavahana Sanchika, Guntur (1950) (Telugu)

" : Buddha Jayanti Souvenir, Supplement (1956)

" : Satavahana Commemoration Volume (1950)

" : Nagarjunakonda Souvenir, Guntur

" : The Kakatiyas of Warangal, Hyderabad

" : The Ikshvakus of Vijayapuri, Tirupati

K. Laksmi Ranjanam: Andhrula Samskriti, Charitra (Telugu)

Burgess: Buddhist Stupas of Amaravati and Jaggayyapeta

V. Yasoda Devi: Women in the Satavahana Empire—pp. 55-59 —Sahiti Vallabhyamu Part I, Narendra Sahityamandali, Tanuku, (1960) Telugu

" : The Chalukyas in Andhradesa—Seminar proceedings volume of the Chalukyas of Kalyani (1976), Bangalore

" : After the Kakatiyas (1975), Hyderabad

" : The Reddis of Kondavidu and Rajahmundry (unpublished)

" : The history of Andhra Desa AD 1000-1500—Subsidiary Dynasties—Journal of Andhra Historical Research Society, Volumes 17 to 27, Rajahmundry

" : Indian History and Culture, Vol. I (1971) Hyderabad (Telugu)

" : Women's Education in Andhra Pradesh, Progress of Women's Education in Free India (Ed) N.B. Sen, New Delhi 1969

" : Gandhian Ideals about Indian Womanhood, Development of Women's Education in New India (Ed) N.B. Sen, New Delhi, 1969

" : Social and Religious Reform Movements in Andhra Pradesh in the 19th and 20th centuries, Social and Religious Reform Movements in the 19th and 20th centuries (Ed) S.P. Sen (1979) Calcutta

N. Ramesan: The Eastern Chalukyas of Vengi (1975) Hyderabad

M.K. Gandhi: Women and Social Injustice

A. Vaidehi: Andhradesa: Women (1975) Hyderabad (Telugu)

Annie Besant: Wake up India

A. Suryakumari: The Temple in Andhradesa (Madurai) 1982

D. Virayya (Ed): Gunturumandala Sarvasvamu (1959) Guntur (Telugu)

N. Chandrasekhara Reddi (Ed): Vikramasimhapuri Mandalasarvasvamu

K. Viresalingam: Autobiography (Telugu)

V.R. Narla: Viresalingam, New Delhi (1968)

Sarojini Regani: Highlights of Freedom Struggle in Andhra Pradesh (1978) Hyderabad

M. Venkatarangayya: Freedom struggle in Andhra Pradesh, Hyderabad

K.K. Datta: Dawn of Renascent India (Bombay) 1904

S. Natarajan: A Century of Social Reform

C.Y. Chintamani (Ed): Indian Social Reform, 1901, Madras

R.C. Majumdar (Ed): History and Culture of the Indian People Vol. IX

" : The British Paramountcy and Indian Renaissance Vol. XI

Sankar Sen Gupta (Ed): Women in Indian Folklore (1970), Calcutta

S.P. Sen (Ed): Social Contents of Indian Religious Reform Movements (1978) Calcutta

Annie Besant: Wake up, India, A plea per Social Reform (1913), Adayar Madras

N. Subba Rao (Ed): Hindu Social Progress (1904), Madras

6

THE URGENT NEED FOR LITERACY AMONG INDIAN WOMEN

Ms Kabita Barua

ON THE threshold of the 21st century India is gearing up modernisation. The progress is impressive in industrial and agricultural sector, but socially we have not been able to keep up with the pace. In the most vital field which is education, nearly 437 million of the population are illiterate and of this 250 million are women. Today, lack of education is a curse on nation which is on its way to advancement. Therefore to bring about total improvement of all citizens it is very important to eradicate illiteracy among women and draw them to the mainstream. The task indeed is challenging, but not impossible. Society outlook towards women must change and they must be respected as individual, and also modern individuals, need in food, shelter, clothing, health and education. The drive for eradication of illiteracy must, therefore, be a top-priority issue not only of the government and social institution, but, of every educated and conscious citizen of our country.

To understand this neglect of women, and the stagnancy in their literacy we have to go through the annals of history of India. From the Indus Valley period till today, the female energy has always been worshipped as a source of evation and destroyer of evils (Goddess Durga). In the Rig Vedic or Early Aryan Period women were not only highly educated but some like Visvakhara, Uppala and Ghosha composed some 'mantras' of the famous Rig Veda. But, in the later Aryan Period the status of women declined yet their education was not neglected. Then gradually the caste system became rigid and education became the right of the members of the upper-caste. A superstitious feeling developed among the majority of Hindu families that, if a girl learns to read and write, after marriage she will become a widow. Others, regarded education of women as an immodest act. Then the dawn of New India saw an illustrious personality in Raja Rammohan Roy, who, apart from his other reforms took up the cause of Indian women, their emancipation, and emphasised their education. The impetus given by him was later carried on by leaders like Ishwar Chandra Vidyasagar, Behramji M. Malahasi, Mahatma Gandhi, Rabindranath Tagore etc. But, unfortunately, even after thirty-nine years of independence the percentage of literate female is just about 25. The British have left, now who do we blame—but ourselves!

Sociologically, though a woman is in the pivotal position of her family, societies in many parts of India still neglect her, and give her a low status. The Indian men have failed to realise that she is not just a wife, mother and confidant of her children but an individual with a mind of her own. To develop this individuality in our women, we have to provide them with formal education, which, as we simply define is the knowledge of three R's (reading, writing, and arithematic) and three L's (looking, listening and learning). If we think for a moment we will know that without education we would be like a rudderless ship on a turbulent sea, yet, we have neglected our women and allowed illiteracy rate among them to increase instead of decreasing.

The importance of education must be immediately infused in the minds of our women. Since every Indian woman gives utmost importance to her family, she should be made aware of the link between benefits of education and her family. It is extremely vital for her to know that once she conceives, the foetus that grows in her work depends on her for its physical as well as mental development. Unlike what many of us think, the learning process starts much early, than the child leaves for school. In this period, the youngster acquired education through informal means and from its mother, father, brother, sister and other. Nevertheless, it is the mother who spends most time tending, slaying and ever talking to the child. This way it learns about life and the environment around its small world. The foundation period should never be overlooked, because, it is private time and the mother consciously or unconsciously influences the mind of her child. Like a potter who moulds mound of clay on its wheel into various shapes and sizes; a mother too moulds the minds and helps build the character of her child. Also, researchers today strongly stress the tremendous influence that parents have on the young minds before they leave for school. The fact is that the inherent potential of each and every child varies and parents must recognise, and, then carefully nuture and nourish it by giving proper encouragement and support. Another thing they ought to scrow is that intelligence is not equal in all children—some acquire through proper guidance and others inherit it. Of course, parents have to enhance it carefully and consciencely by giving law and understanding. What it clearly shows is that education today is first indispensable for both parents and their children, or else they will be vulnerable beings in this highly technologically advancing world.

Sadly enough, in our ceuntry the girl child is still neglected. Her birth brings gloom to the family rather than joy. What a welcome, indeed, to an innocent being! Her brother on one hand is showered with love and care and given proper food while she is burdened with domestic chores like looking after the baby, fetching water, collecting firewood and even grazing cattle. At a stage when she should be playing with dolls, live in a fantasy world and study in schools, her family makes her watch for their economic wellbeing, soon after a girl is born to majority of Indian families, parents begin saving money, jewellery, clothes, household commodities etc. to give as dowry to the groom on her marriage. These age-old customs which are still prevalent have kept alive the misconception that a girl is a binder on her family. But what is disappointing, is that, the middle-class people of whom most how, atleast, some education also do not encourage higher education for girls and they rather invest that money for her marriage. Thus, educational syllabus must be comprehensive and adaptable to that environment, it must include vocational education to make the girls and women independent for 37 per cent (according to Governments, statistics) of our population still live below the poverty line.

Our progress in the field of politics, culture, economics will be meaningless if illiteracy prevails in our society. At the moment, out of every hundred Indian woman only twenty-five are literate and the rest seventy-five are illiterate. This negligence is proving expensive and therefore literacy must be made complusory for every citizen of this country. Basically our character has not changed and through media, A.I.R. and Doordarshan we keep hearing regularly of social crimes especially dowry-deaths which has become such a common feature that most of us are hardly affected by such gruesome acts, we sign and forget; corruption is rampant in almost every nook and corner of the country; occasional commercial riots disrupt normalcy and creates tension and suspicion among different groups of people; rise of pacticularism in some parts of the country will certainly make our country vulnerable to external forces not-to-speak of the tragedy within it that it created with loss of valuable innocent lives, property etc. The solution, of course, will be to make education suitable for everyone including woman. It is the woman who can teach her child to be a better citizen with a good character. Through education if mothers can build the characters of their children, they will will be in turn changing our national character for they are tomorrow's citizen.

While we speak of providing education we should not only concentrate on girl-child's education and overlook the middle-aged and aged women. These women too must be educated for we want an alround progress. Adult education centre must be opened at all available places and mostly near the homes of these women so that they don't have to come far away from home to such centres. The timing at these centres should vary according to their suitability and also be provided with toys and other ammenities to keep the children who accompany their mouths engaged.

Social biases, prevented due to illiteracy, in our country has led to the neglect of woman's health among low-income group women and these residing in rural areas. Get these women work for larger duration than men and along with men they too work in hazardous condition like mines, construction sites etc. where the barest safety measures are not taken. Even those who work in agricultural field suffer from backache while they tend to ignores. Let alone the society even their families hardly better about their health. An average pregnant woman of this country receives hardly any ante-natal or post-natal care which leads to infant mortality and other complications. Illiteracy and improper education are together the root cause for the still existing preference for male child. This has led to frequent pregnancies among many unfortunate women who to give birth to baby boy have neglected their own health. On the other hand the indication is that female infant mortality is high during early years of their birth because of inadequate nourishment and neglect in their health care. Our women due to their lack of education have become guinea-pigs for contraceptive research. And now amniocentesis have become a big business in most of our leading cities. Women undergoing these tests are not informed of the risks musling the mother and the foetus. Also, we cannot feign ignorance at the destruction of thousands of femal foetuses that are going on in India. But where literacy rate is high as in the state of Kerala, infant mortality is low. Therefore, we have to see that the right to education is not denied to our women who are and would be mothers of the luture generation.

The impact of illiteracy is being felt even in our environment. The thoughtless felling of trees has led to the destruction of beautiful forests, once heaven of rare kinds, wild life, trees and flowers. In the arid zone our-grazing have led to desertification of more lands. Many parts of India are experiencing weather changes which have been unknown in those regions like for example drought in Assam which usually enjoys abundant rainfall. Yearly growth of population creates pressure on land for cultivation, shelter and livelihood. Also pollution is increasing mainly in the cities and towns. Little do we realise that air pollution, sound pollution, water pollution are all affecting our health. The motive of education should be made to make our people aware that if we care for our environment it will reciprocate by giving us rain for cultivation, water to drink, the greenery which purifies the air, the wonderful kinds and wild-animals and the exotic flora.

Lately national integration has become an important topic for our country. Particuliasm and communalism are raising their ugly heads in various parts of the country. A secular nation like India has people belonging to different religions residing and we cannot and should not shed blood about petty differences among us. Another cause of worry that many of us are not aware of is particuliasm which will in turn create not a united but a disunited and shattered India. Through education we have to open the eyes of our people as to how interested foreign powers are playing with own emotions and taking full advantage of our ignorant and innocent masses. Then we will not need bannas, advertisements and cultural utsavas for bringing about unity in diversity, because then it will come out spontaneously from our masses.

The challenge to eradicate illiteracy among our women masses is a tough one. But it can be conquered through determination, motivation, sincerity and cooperation especially among the educated women to educate those unfortunate women. As we know, the task ahead is not all that simple because we will be coming against odds and barriers from the society and women who have been very much used to being neglected and are afraid to venture out. It will definitely need patience and perseverence and we should not lose heart at initial obstacles. The Government on its part should make basic formal education compulsory. Vocational education must be part of the curriculum to make women independent economically and mentally. This will also benefit the economic condition of the families of low-income groups who will then automatically encourage education among the girls and women of the family. But what is most important in impartation of education is the syllabus. On it depends the national character of our masses, because as we can see for ourselves that high demand for dowry are made by I.A.S., I.P.S., doctors, engineers etc. who are well-educated. Syllabus should be comprehensive and adaptable to different situation. Schools and adult education centres should be increased so that girls and women do not have to go far to study, and, of course, the time-table should be made in such a way so that it does not clash with their domestic chores. Everything possible must be provided with, to bring out the women to schools. We are emphasising the urgent need for literacy among women because the education of our future generation at the foundation level is at their hands. Indeed Nehruji had very rightly said, "Education of a boy is education of one person, but education of a girl is education of the entire family". We do not have much time in hand and peace without wasting anymore time. We must mobilise our human and economic resources to educate our illiterate female mass with devotion and hard work and we will surely achieve our goal.

7

ECONOMIC AND PHYSICAL EXPLOITATION OF TRIBAL FEMALE LABOURERS

DR (MRS) SUSHAMA SAHAY PRASAD

THE disadvantages experienced by women in rural areas and their handicaps in becoming equal partners in development have emerged as critical issues in all countries including India, where a vast majority of women are in the rural areas.

Women play a vital role in the rural economy of India. However, their socio-economic status remain marginal. There exists a segregation within the female labour market which is determined by social hierarchy, caste, ethnic groups, etc. About 18 per cent of the total labour in India is female representing around 12 per cent of the female population. Over half the rural female workers are landless agricultural labourers, 33 per cent are self-employed in agricultural enterprises, and 4 per cent in household enterprises.

Indian women are not a homogeneous group. Their traditional roles are not identical in all strata of society. Norms and taboos governing their roles and behaviour within and outside the family, the patterns of family organisations and social practices and the positions accorded to women in a community differ considerably across regions, cultures and levels of socio-economic development.[1]

In the tribal societies women contribute to the working force in a more substantial way than in the non-tribal society. While the ratio between the male and female workers in the general population of the country is 5:1; it is 3:1 among the tribal people. Among the non-tribal women 11.9 per cent are workers whereas their tribal sisters have 20.75 per cent as workers. The comparative figures of the participation rate of the non-tribal in the different sectors of economy are given below.

Comparative figures of the participation rate of non-tribals and tribal female workers in different sectors

Primary Sector

Occupational	*Cultivation*	*Agricultural Laboures*	*Mining*	*Livestock, Forestry, Fishing, hunting, etc.*
1	*2*	*3*	*4*	*5*
General Female	29.8%	50.5%	0.4%	2.5%
Tribal Female	42.7%	48.9%	0.6%	2.6%

Secondary Sector

Occupational categories	*Household industries*	*Manufacturing etc.*	*Construction*
1	*2*	*3*	*4*
General Female	4.3%	2.8%	0.7%
Tribal Female	1.3%	0.9%	0.3%

(*Contd.*)

Tertiary Sector

Occupational categories	*Trade and Commerce*	*Transport etc.*	*Other services*
1	*2*	*3*	*4*
General Female	1.8%	0.5%	—
Tribal Female	0 6%	0.2%	—

Since the tribal economy is largely confined to the primary sector, 90.6 per cent of the female workers are engaged in agriculture, as cultivators or as labourers, 2.67 per cent in pastoralism, hunting, etc. and 0.6 per cent in mining and quarring.

Although the tribal males are still the major breadwinners in the families, in recent times the economic contribution of the tribal women has assumed significant role due to various reasons. On account of the operation of a large number of factors, such as the opening of the tribal country, growing industrialisation, growth of education and the impact of christianity, opportunities for diversification of occupation as well as social mobility have multiplied. The building up of roads and development of fast communication have led to a large number of tribal women taking to petty trading and other income generating activities like vegetable selling, working as maid servants, casual and agricultural labour. In tribal areas where a lot of constructional activities and industrial operations are being carried out such as, in the state of Bihar, Madhya Pradesh, West Bengal, Orissa, tribal women have been drawn in the unskilled labour force. The tribal women now even migrate outside their villages, district and state for periods ranging from 2 to 6 months for working in the brick-kilns, agricultural fields, tea-estates, etc.

The tribal women get attracted to such employment avenues as it gives them ready cash with which they can buy new dress, cheap ornaments and trinkets. They also enjoy the daily outing. But, in many of the industrial centres the employment of tribal women have led to several forms of physical and economic exploitations. The freedom enjoyed by the tribal women in their own social system has been mistaken for licence by the alien contractors and non-tribals who utilise them for their own economic gains and satisfying their carnal desires. Thus, economic exploitation unavoidably paves way for physical exploitation; and to be more precise sexual exploitation.[2]

This essay seeks to highlight the various forms of economic and physical exploitations which the tribal female labourers have to undergo while working in construction sites, brick kilns, etc. The data for this essay were collected during the author's doctoral research in the district of Ranchi, Bihar state, India. In all 300 tribal female labourers working in construction sites, brick kilns, transport companies and industrial complexes etc. were interviewed to understand the various exploitative process working against them. In what follows an attempt has been made to discuss briefly the economic and physical exploitation of the tribal female labourers.

The tribals living in Ranchi district are either landless or marginal cultivators. Even the land possessed by the tribals are infertile and lack irrigational facilities. Whatever good pieces of agricultural land that exist in the tribal belt of Ranchi district somehow or other, have been grabbed by the non-tribals. As a result of these constraints not only the marginal cultivators but the smaller ones also can hardly manage to eak out a subsistence from agriculture for more than 5 to 6 months in a year. Thus, in the lean periods, the tribals mostly eke out their living by working as labourers. The month of October-November is mostly a difficult period for the tribals because they are not only left without any work in agricultural fields but also find their food-stock completely exhausted.

In the tribal societies males and females are equally responsible for earning towards the maintenance of family. But when they find that they are facing difficulties in respect of procuring food to eat at village level, they set out in search of work to places other than their villages. Some tribal males and females not only go beyond the boundry of their village, block, subdivision and district levels but also beyond the State boundaries order to ward off starvation.

For the tribals of Ranchi winter is a time when they face their recurring choice between starvation and brutal exploitation. Man and nature together mock at them during this season. Natural calamities drive them out of their villages in the look out for cheap labour. In the tribal belt of Ranchi the land is undulating and acidic and hence the productivity is at the lowest ebb. The agricultural season is short (between June and October) and runs out soon after the monsoon ends. The little usufructs which they have are hypothicated to the *Sahus* (money lenders) against earlier incurred loans. There are no irrigational facilities, electricity or proper roads and thus the tribals can produce only one crop annually at the utmost. And the forest land, which belongs to the government, is also out of bounds for the poor tribals, the government contracts out the forest land to the highest bidder.

Besides this, parts of the tribal belts of Ranchi have been occupied by industrialists and trading communities for commercial interests because the areas are full of minerals and raw materials. Moreover entrepreneurs get tax and other reliefs for "developing" these forlorn areas. But for the tribals this has simply meant loss of land and the compensation that has been paid to them amounted to paltry sums. They have also not been favoured with jobs created under the new projects. The tribals can only provide unskilled labour which is supplied by contractors who prefer to bring in labourers from outside because they can be easily manipulated in areas remote and unfamiliar. Besides, the closer of certain mines and factories in Ranchi district drove many tribal families to face starvation. This scenario, which made the entire area a depot of cheap labour, is ideal for labour agents, brick-kiln owner, etc. who wait to engage such helpless labourers.

Every year, around September, agents of brick kiln owners come to the tribal belt in search of cheap labour. As soon as they arrive they establish contacts with *sardars* and *sardarnis*, local sub-agents, who are themselves tribals and have worked for many years in brick-kilns. There are more *sardarnis* than *sardars* and most of the people recruited from this region are women. These sub-agents, who are paid Rs. 30 to Rs. 40 for each labourer they can find, set about contacting the local tribal people. Once recruited, the tribals are paid *dadoon* or advance, usually between Rs. 100 to Rs. 150, and towards the end of October they are herded to the railway station (their fare is paid by the agents). Once the tribals reach the brick kiln they are categorised and work begins. The job of carrying bricks from where they are moulded to the furnaces where they are baked is usually done by women and children, known as *rejas*. Work begins at sunrise and ends at sunset, for six days a week. And for all this work the pay is abysmally low. For carrying ten unbaked bricks at a time to a distance of 300 to 350 metres to the furnace, the *reja* receives one *tickly* (token). Twenty such tokens fetch one rupee. For carrying baked bricks the rate is even less: one rupee for carrying about 400 bricks over the same distance. As a result the most a *reja* can earn is Rs. 4 a day or Rs. 24 for the week. But even this amount is not paid in whole to the *reja*. Out of the total weekly earning only some money to buy the bare necessities is paid while the rest amount is withheld by the Munshi (manager) on the pretext to be paid it afterwards.

Since the wage payments are made to the tribal female labourers by employer's agents, a part of the wage is always witheld so that the labourers remain in the grip of the labour agents or contractors. The labour agents care only for their own interests. But on the contrary less payments made to the labourers result in their economic exploitation which in turn lead to physical exploitation. The contractors and the employers always take extra work from the female labourers by asking them to work beyond the normal working hour. What is actually done is that the contractors call them to start work much before the actual time and compell them to work much beyond the closing hours by giving wrong time to the labourers. The female labourers hardly understand the meaning of normal working hours per day and in the absence of knowledge of time keeping mechanism the contractors mercilessly extract much more work from them. Although extra work is frequently taken from the female labourers by their employers, they are seldom paid for the additional labour rendered by them. Thus by taking work beyond the normal working hour and not making payment for this additional work the employers are economically and physically exploiting the tribal female labourers.

Not only the tribal female labourers working in the brick kilns suffer physical and economic exploitations at the hands of their employers, but even the female labourers working in construction work, transportation compaines, etc. are also subjected economic and physical exploitations by their employers and contractors. The labour contractors act as intermediaries between the management and the female labourers and insist on the management to make payments according to the Minimum Wages Act. But the contractors themselves do not give minimum wages to the labourers in general and female labourers in particular. The female labourers have no protection or affiliation with any recognised labour and trade unions. As a result they find nobody who could understand their problems and protect them from economic and physical exploitations.

The accommodation provided for the tribal female labourers working at different labour centres is not only inadequate but also unhygienic. The female labourers are quartered in four feet by five feet *Jhopris* (huts) which are about four feet high. No labourer can sleep in such huts without their legs protruding through the open door. Besides, there are no arrangements for drinking water and there are no toilets. Medical facilities are missing. However, some labour centres were found to be equipped with first-aid kits, but there number is very small. Again, as the brick and other such industries where tribal female labourers work, do not fall under the purview of the Factory Act, Employees State Insurance (ESI) facilities are not extended to these labours.

But the greatest humiliation that the tribal female labourers have to suffer is that of sexual exploitation. It is not uncommon for a tribal female labourer to be locked up and beaten up if she refuses to yield sexually to her employer of local toughs. Apart from being raped by contractors, young tribal girls have to face same fate at the hands of local hoodlooms. Sometimes even the *sardarnis* (female labour agents) force tribal girls into prostitution. The labour contractors and the employers think that the tribal female labourers do not have any character as they drink and dance and can sleep with any one for a small favour.

The economic and physical exploitation of unorganised labour force in general and female labour force in particular is not a new phenomenon. State and Central Government have framed several rules and enacted legislations to check the exploitative forces. But there has been a staggering gap between the framing rules, enacting legislations and their effective implementation. The tribal women who have been drawn into the unorganised labour force for about past two decads are in process of striking a balance between their economic problems, which force them to accept the drudgeries of unorganised labour employment, and the exploitative, both economic and physical, forces. Unless the various labour laws and Acts are made leak-proof, the unorganised labor, including the tribal female labourers, would continue to be economically and physically exploited.

REFERENCES

1. Sachchidananda, "Social Structure, Status and Mobility Pattern: The Case of Tribal Women," *Man in India*, Vol. 58, No. 1, January-March, 1978.
2. *Ibid.*

8

STATUS OF WOMEN CONSTRUCTION WORKERS IN DEVELOPING COUNTRIES: AN INDIAN STUDY

SMT. SHUBHANGI G. GOTE-GARHANE

INTRODUCTION

STATUS of unorganised female workforce in developing societies is of peculiar character in nature as they constitute majority of the workforce, and also most neglected one in the male-dominated societies. "The Census of India 1971 returned 31 million women as workers. As many as 29 million, *i.e.* 94 per cent of the total female workforce is engaged in the unorganised sector, 81.4 per cent in agriculture and the rest in non-agricultural occupations. While some data are available regarding agricultural workers, information on non-agricultural occupations in the unorganised sector is scanty and not very reliable" (G.P. Shinde, S.N. Ranade—1975). Among the non-agricultural sector unorganised female workforce women construction workers are not studied yet from sociological point of view.

Women construction workers' is a significant group of women in unorganised sector of India. National Committee on "Status of Women in India" has made following observations:

"Out of 31 million women return as workers by 1971 Census, 25 millions were in agriculture and about two millions in the organised sector. We have therefore, estimated that remaining four millions were in non-agricultural occupations in the unorganised sector and suffered from insecurity of employment, lack of standard minimum wages, excessive hours of work and absence of any welfare aminities" (R.N. Sachdev, 1974). As the women from this unorganised category do not enjoy any facilities or amenities as the workers in the organised sector enjoy. As these women are unorganised, naturally they are not able to better their working conditions nor they are able to better their life situation. The number of women in the construction industry is substantial. "The number of women in this industry, according to the Census 1971 was 0.2 million as against two million men. Women workers constitute 9.2 per cent of the total workers in this industry in India. Since the majority of construction workers are either contract or casual labour, the problem of ensuring minimum protection and security for them has proved to be an extremely difficult task" (G. P. Sinha, S. N. Ranade—(1975). So the research work was undertaken by the present research on the topic "Sociological Study of Women Construction Workers" for the award of M. Phil degree. This essay is based on the M. Phil. dissertation of the researcher.

The purpose of studying these women construction workers was to see whether these women belonging to lower class are enjoying the benefits of democracy or modernisation.

METHODOLOGY

Women construction workers in Aurangabad city were chosen for this study. Aurangabad is divisional headquarter of backward region of Maharashtra State (India). So universe was women construction workers in Aurangabad city. As the absence of a list of construction workers, purposive sampling technique was used. As the sampling was purposive one, researcher approached women construction workers, wherever they were found on the site. Information was collected from one hundred respondents; with the help of highly structured interview schedule as the respondents were illiterate. The nature of the research work was formulative one. Information was collected on the familial aspect, work condition, socio-political life, economic condition, religious life etc. Entire data were coded and hand processed. As the research was formulative in nature, and there were lack of data, researcher could not frame definitive hypothesis.

PERSONAL AND FAMILIAL ASPECT OF W.C.W.D.

Most strikingly, it is revealed by the analysis of the data collected, that this most neglected women labour force, is far away from the impact and benefits of modernisation and social policy, inspite of living in the city like Aurangabad. Considering the agewise breakup of the respondents, 80 per cent were within the age group of 15 to 38 years. It means most of the women coustruction workers were young.

Distribution according to caste indicated that 75 per cent of total respondents were from Scheduled Caste, 6 per cent belonging to Scheduled Tribe in India *i.e.* 81 per cent were belonging to the downtrodden and unpriviledged castes. Only 6 per cent were from upper caste named "Maratha." Ester Boserup has pointed paralleled observations "Both in Indian rural areas and in the towns, the female construction workers are tribal and low caste women of rural origin" (Ester Boserup, 1970). In this study 79 per cent respondents were having rural origin and they were migrated to the Aurangabad city. Educational status of these women was found contrary to the literacy rate of the India. Among the total respondents 97 per cent were illiterates (32 per cent being the national literacy rate of India). 2 per cent were having only primary education and none of them could go through the Secondary School Examination (S.S.C.).

TABLE 1

Age of marriage

Age of marriage	*Frequency*
5—10 years	42%
11—16 years	55%
17—22 years	02%
Total	99%

Almost all women construction workers were got married before attaining 16 year of age. Only two of them *i.e.* 2 per cent were married within the age limit of 17-22. The present researcher had come across the frightening bare reality of Indian Society that 92 per cent of respondents were married below the age of 16 years, against lawful marriage age for female in India being minimum 18 years. It was more stricking to note the rate of child marriage prevalent among these female construction workers, 42 per cent of the women married before attaining the 10 years of age. The incidence of child-marriage among women construction workers shows that dominating role played by traditionalism on their lives.

Most of the husband's of these women were also construction workers (80 per cent with 69 per cent of them were illiterate and 79 per cent were habituated to tobacco and 'beedi'). Analysis of the data collected indicates that 70 per cent of the respondents were having 4 children and girls 9 per cent were having 5 when Government of India propagates limit of 'only two' most of these poverty-ridden women were having 'double' than the limit. Small children for the women worker is always liability. It becomes very difficult to work outside, when children are small or under the age of six. The present researcher found that 40 per cent respondents were having small children and they were taking them at the site of the work. It was observed that there were no amenities of child care, no cradle arrangements were made by the employers for looking after and keeping their small children at work site. Researcher Tara Ali Baig has made some observation: "In construction work which has mashroomed in the last two decades in all big cities, contractors feel no responsibility for care of babies though they employ large numbers of women for carrying and coolie work. The babies consequently lie about on sandpiles, earth or stones which become dusty, dangerous playground for toddlers, and a nearby tree serves as a cradle with father's turban tied to the branches from which the youngest dangles" (Tara Ali Baig, 1976). It is also noteworthy that 59 per cent of respondents were doing their household work before and after the work. If parental occupation is seen, it was found that 34 per cent parents were in construction industry and 57 per cent were doing the farm work, *i.e.* 91 per cent parents of these women construction workers were belonging to the toiling labour class, living in the huts.

DIFFERENT FACETS OF WOMEN CONSTRUCTION WORKERS

As these women construction workers have to work outside more than eight houses, they have to complete household work before they start for their work outside. 89 per cent of the respondents were getting up before 5 a.m. and were used to do household work after returning from the work till late in the night. Similar situation is pointed out in the study of Karnataka State (India) "quite often they have to complete several other work including cooking and leave home quite early. After the work they return home tired and then attend to the household work. This has to be done on a routine basis" (Mumtaz Ali Khan Noor Aysha, 1982). Naturally these most sufferer class of women workforce, due to their strenuous nature of work 81 per cent of respondents were facing pains in different parts of the body.

It is revealed from the data collected that they were deprived from even religious activities. Religion seems to be luxury of the higher classes. These poor women had no time even to worship or go to the temple every day, their entire life seems to be working life.

TABLE 2

Whether worship daily or not

Answer		*Frequency*
Yes	...	0.6%
No	...	0.9%
Only on the day of festival	...	85%
Total	...	100%

It is observed that 70 per cent of the respondents could not spare time for going temple every day. 26 per cent were able to visit the temple only on festival day. It means 96 percent of the respondents were unable to spare few minutes for visiting temple from their over-tight burden on working day. It is also found that these unpriviledged women force is restricted by their socio-economic conditions in visiting pilgrimage centres. It is naked reality that inspite of their religious interests, 83 per cent of respondents could not be able to visit the pilgrimage centres.

Even more shocking is the fact that the recreational activities were also luxury for them. We have general impression that in India, most of the masses of lobour force has films as their only recreational item. But these female women construction workers were found also deprived from even seeing films. It is most tragic on their part that 96 per cent of the respondents were unable to spare time for seeing films. This is nothing but their cultural exploitation.

While considering their political life, it is found that most of these women said that they exercised their vote in the elections. According to the dictation of their menfolk 89 per cent respondents were found not giving vote voluntarily. It is clear from this observation that mandate of masses in India is male-dominated and women of lower classes are not even having autonomy of franchise in the democracy. Coming to the political awareness of these women construct workers it is found that they were unaware of the Chief Minister of their respective State *i.e.* Maharashtra State (100 per cent frequency). Only political leader they were knowing was late Prime Minister Smt. Indira Gandhi. This indicates that these women were less-informed by mass media. This communication age is found even in respect of beneficial legislature measures have not reached up to them. As most of these women were illiterate, they were not aware of 'minimum wage Act,' also they were not aware of the discrimination which the employers do for male and female workers. It is observed that 100 per cent discrimination was existing in the wage rate of male and female workers. Yoder observed that "It ascertained that female workers are paid much less than what the male workers are paid." (Dale Yoder, 1939). It means that situation has not changed at all since 1940's. 99 per cent of these women were getting daily wages less than 7 rupees appropriately. 92 per cent were unsatisfied with their wages. They were not having their trade union, no security of work, no weekly holiday, nothing except exploitation in all possible manners.

CONCLUSIONS

1. Normally these women work for 8-9 hours a day at the site with less than Rs. 7 as daily wage rate, nature of work being casual.
2. These women workers were belonging to the socially and economically unpriviledged castes, migrated from rural agricultural labour families.
3. These women were unaware of political, social and economical legitimate rights provided to them by welfare state.
4. These women were unable to spare time for religious recreational activities.

5. These women workforce was found living in subhuman level of minimum standard of living.

So conclusion can be made by these observations that even-after 35 years of independence these women still belong to weaker section of the society. Independence, modernisation of urban life has not brought any change in their lives. This shows that constitutional and legislative measures benefiting the e class have not reached to them. Few legislative measures and so-called constitutional gurantee of better life are just on paper and not in practice. These are naked indicators about status of women workers in developing societies of their multifaceted sub-human status, far away from the basic human rights and fruits of modernisation, social policy measures.

REFERENCES

1. Shinde G. P. S. N. Ranade "Women in a Developing Economy-2 Women Construction Workers"—Reports of the two surveys, Allied Publishers Pvt. Ltd., Bombay-38, 1975 (ICSSR).
2. Sachdev R. N. "Status of Women in India"—A synopsis of the report of the National Committee, Allied Publishers Pvt. Ltd., 1971-74, (ICSSR).
3. Ester Boserup: "Women's Role in Economic Development" Aberdeon University, George Alien and Unwin Ltd., London, 1970.
4. Tara Ali Baig "India's Women Power", S. Chand and Co. Pvt. Ltd., New Delhi, 1976.
5. Mumtaz Ali Khan Noor Aysha, "Status of Rural Women in India" —A Study of Karnataka, B. S. Uppal Publishing House, New Delhi, 1982.

9

RE-DISCOVERY OF SPIRITUALISM IN INDIAN WOMANHOOD

MRS JAYASREE BANERJEE

"Mother from the unreal lead us to the Real,
from darkness lead us unto light,
from death lead us unto immorality,
Reach us through and through ourself
And evermore protect us, on thou terrible;
From ignorance, by thy
Sweet compassionate face."

IT IS the most attractive ideal of Hindu philosophy in India, the mother is the centre of the family and our highest ideal.

She is to us the representative of God, as God—is the mother of the Universe.[1] The end of marriage is something spiritual rather than personal pleasure. Here she is essentially not the object of man's last but is the mother, the maker, the leader. It is the opportunity of a mother to help her children to develop the destinctive gifts, physical and mental, ethical and spiritual:

> "Matri devo bhava—treat your mother as a Goddess—is the advice given to the Young."[2]
>
> "Dark mother; Always gliding near with soft feet,
> Have none chanted for
> Thee a Chant of fullest
> Welcome?
>
> WALT WHITEMAN

Today the world is now full of problems—the problem of war, food, establishment etc. Inspite of this we believe it is the mother who has the capacity to bring the Golden Corn before her children and have the power to stop the war and make the land an abode of peace. It is said that the youths and the mothers of U.S.A. stopped the Vietnam War.

In India we have a great respect for motherhood. Manu declares that God bless those families where women are happy and well treated.[3] To realise the ideal of Indian womanhood as holly mother we must have to study the evolution of the feminine ideal in India from the ancient times.

In the Vedic age women enjoyed equal opportunities for education and work. The tenth mandala of the Rig Veda Samhita—represented the eternal glory of Indian womanhood. Here a lady—daughter of the Sage Ambhirna—through self-illumination she realised her complete identity with the Great One (Brahman) and says 'it is I who string the bow of Rudra'[4] that was the Vedic woman's ideal which was chanted 5,000 years ago. Afterwards we come to the Upanishadic Age, another ideal of Indian Womanhood—the Brahmavadinis, Women who sought and spoke of Brahman. Important among them were Maitry and Gargi.

Maitrayee refused to take property from her husband Yajnavalkya are said 'What shall I do with that which will not make me immortal'?[5] In an assembly of a 1,000 thousand Brahmans experts in the Vedas, Gargi boldly challenged Yajnavalkya in a discussion about Brahma.[6] History repeats itself. All nations have attained greatness by paying proper respect to women—the living images of Shakti.

The Epic period philosophy is a transition between the period of Upanishads and that of the later systems. A compromise between the ancient and new theories. The poetry of Epics proves the attitude of the Hindu mind towards problems of higher thought and wisdom. Ultimate goal of life expressed in various aspects—Nirvana (free), Ananda (Pleasure) and Amrita (immortality). It is Mahabharata for the first time the liberal doctrine teaches of emancipation which do not bother for the barrier of caste, creed, or sex. We have women philosophers like Sulava, Pingala who were the worthy teachers of religion and philosophy. The Epic teachings help to satisfy the frustrated human mind, for example we can refer the case of Pingala—calmly sleeps after renouncing her desire, wishes and hopes.

India says "Show your power by suffering" for the race. Sita of Ramayan stands as the ideal of suffering. She is typical of Indian woman—the idealised woman. She stands for everything that is good, pure and holy. She is the ideal of God. She is glorious, purer, symbol of all patience and suffering.

So Swamiji said the women of the India must grow and develope in the footprints of Sita and that is the only way.[7] She is the true representation of forbearance and courage. The partisans of her land challenged the holiness of her secret character, demanded examination through fire. Sita refused and upholding her self respect prayed to mother Basumati—who gave her the real asylam. Thus Sita showed that she did not bother for any ephimeral wealth and pleasure. She dedicated her life for the sake of her lord and children and for the welfare of the country, partisans too. Thus she inspired the women of the world even modern too—to be free from bondage and slavery. She refused to submit before the long views of her holy character and maintained her personality and own characteristics.

Another spirited woman of India was Savitri, whose love could not be conquered by death and with this great love she brought back the soul of her husband even from Yama. So Swamiji said the ideal woman will be pure like Sita and Arundhati, received proper respects like revered risis of the vedic ages, bold like Savitri and Draupadi—saved the Pancha-pandav when they lost everything in the dice play and Bhramba-badini like Gargi and Maitri.

This is the ideal. The ideal of constancy, the ideal of purity, which is the distinguishing feature of the Indian Ethos, though we are forgetting it gradually.[8]

Coming down to the historical times we meet some women symbolising another ideal, the ideal of martial heroism. Remarkable among them was the Rani of Jhansi.

The other woman was Shivaji's mother, inspired his son to protect the motherland and to fight always, though in defeat that's the ideal. Enjoy the world like a valiant not as a coward or slave—the ideal of Srimad Bhagvat Gita. Another Padmini, the queen of Chittore dedicated her life for the sake of the prestige of Rajput women as well as her motherland etc. All of them present the virtues of chastity and forbearance and courage to face critical situation.

For this Swamiji said "I want our women to be free but not at the cost of their purity."[9] Unfortunately this ideal of purity is lacking in our society. Nevertheless we dreamt like Swamiji who could not think of an Indian woman to be without spirituality. The lady or the house-wife goes to the place of worship, lights the lamp or incense sticks and sits for sometime in Japa and Meditation. This spiritual discipline is an invari-able part of a Hindu woman's life.

The embodiment of such ideal was the Holy Mother—"Sarada Devi". She possessed in herself the noble characteristics of all those great women who proceeded her. She is regarded as the ideal for modern Indian womanhood. The ideals which deal with eternal truths of spiritual life was adopted by her, according to the needs of the contemporary society. She followed every responsibility as a house-holder yet she towered over everything, in the midst of all the troubles of the world. She radiated peace and equanimity and every thing she did was a blessing to others. We observed that nowadays the world is in a tension of an automatic coalition, the culture is in a tension of an automatic coalition, the culture is destructive and decaying. We believe, for its survival as it needs the infusion of spirituality.

For this problem west is looking for India. Here we have the Holy Mother—a source of great consolation and a great ideal for all of us. Of course she is the mother of all, both East and West. "I am your own true mother "—" Think the whole world is yours. No one is Stranger" were her last words and teaching.

Therefore it is our duty to bring for the need of India great fearless women—"Women worthy to continue the tradition of Sanghamitra, Lila, Ahalyabai and Mirabai—Women fit to be mothers of heroes because they are pure and selfless, strong with the strength that comes of touching the feet of God".[10]

Besides by their own spirit, love and devotion to service they will be the great asylum for the world. Men and women must view with sympathy not with antagonism. In the love of the mother in the mutual devotion of man and woman achievements of the world should be guided. It is the duty of an woman who is the "Mother not in the flesh alone but in the spirit . . ." selection also of what is truest and based in the complete aims, ideas and efforts of humanity. The conception applies equally to the racial spirit of motherhood of which the higher abotars of human life are derivative manifestation.[11]

Inspite of so many inconveniences in my motherland I dreamt of an Indian woman—a vision of a Holy Mother.[12]

One girl wearing a Red Bordered Sari and taking a broom-stick in her hand was sweeping the floor. On her waist she carried a pot. Mother asked her, Dear, what are you doing? The girl replied I am sweeping away all vices and evils. Mother then enquired "What then do you have in that pot on your waist"?

She replied that the water of Nectar. I shall bring peace to all being and cool their hearts by sprinkling this over them with tender leaves.

We hope in the present day world the Holy Mother or the Indian woman will play the same role. They will play the role of a peace maker, following the examples of our great mother and images. Our present day woman will have the spirit of self confidence, work as a protective force. She will have that foresight and devotion by which she will help her children to be self sufficient and broad hearted which make our world beautiful and our son will pray:

"Open the Gates of light
O Mother,
To me, Thy tired son,
I long, O long, to return home,
Mother, My play is done."[13]

REFERENCES

1. Detroit Tribune—21st February—Swami Vivekananda.
2. Great Women of India—Advaita Ashram—S. Radhakrishnan, p. XV-XVII.
3. 'Our Women—Swami Vivekananda, Advaita Ashram, p. 11, 1982.
4. —Rick Vedo 10,125.6.
5. —Brihatdaranyaka Upanishad—2.4.2. & 4.5.3.
6. —*Ibid.*, p. 26.
7. —Complete work of Swami Vivekananda—Vol III Edition 9,. pp. 255-256—Advaita Ashram Mayavati.
8. —Article written by Swami Hiranmoyananda—Name of the article the wholly Mother Ideal—Prabudha Bharata, p. 107, March 1985 —Advaita Ashram.
9. *Ibid.*, p. 108.
10. Our Women—Swami Vivekananda. p. 51, Advaita Ashram—1982.
11. Briffeult—The mothers, pp. 520-21.
12. Life of Swami Vireswarananda—Belur Math—1985, p. 40.
13. Swami Vivekananda—My play is done, poem.

SELECT BIBLIOGRAPHY

Great Women of India: Advaita Ashram.
Our Women: Swami Vivekananda.
The Mothers: Briffault.
Cultural Heritage of India: Ramakrishna Mission, Institute of Culture, Golpark, Calcutta.
Article written by Swami Hiranmaya Nanda—Pravudya Bharat —Advaita Ashram,—Mayavati.
Nivedita Lokomata: Sankari Prasad Basu.

10

PROSTITUTION AN INDIAN PERSPECTIVE

DR. A. SURYAKUMARI

PROSTITUTION as profession is a public evil and is considered as a disgrace to civilization. It has been the bane of society and had its origin since the down of civilization. It is still deeply rooted not only in India but also in all the countries of the world. But this institution has never been recognised by society. Society has never recognised it because "it brings in its train not only the personal disorganisation of the persons conerned, but also affects the life organisation of the family and the community at large."[1]

Prostitution may be defined as "the practice of habitual or intermittent sexual union more or less promiscucous, for mercenary inducement".[2] But prositititution is not to be confused with the illicit sex union of lovers because there is no affection in prostitution. Generally it has been defined as promiscuous intercourse for hire whether in money or in kind. The three important elements of prostitution according to C.R. Madan are: (1) illicit and promiscuous sexual intercourse, (2) mercenary basis whether in cash or in kind, and (3) lack of affection or personal interest.[3]

The origin of prostitution is shrouded in mystery. We have absolutely no way of knowing when prostitution in India arose as a baneful profession or how much the prostitute received by way of payment. Its emeregence as a profession was presumably concommitant with the institution of strict marriage rules especially monoardry and the wife being regarded as the private property of her husband.[4]

The process of the origin of prostitution must have been slow, varying from region to region and from age to age. In the primitive society, the prostitutes were considered as a symbol of the prosperity. Like gold and jewellery, corn and cattle, a rich man desired prosperity and plenty in the number of women he could enjoy freely. Soceity considered it as a respectful profession because it served its specific purpose by catering to men's needs of extra marital sexual gratification and also the states' needs by bringing in considerable and secret political information through espionage.

Chief courtesans of prosperous cities and towns maintained their own train of singers and dancing girls. The *Mahabharata* tells us that the Pandava army was followed by a host of prostitutes who went in the rear of the army as baggage courts.[5]

The marriage with the prostitutes was not considered as inferior by the primitive people. In India as in other parts of the world, all sorts of sexual relationship were found with the prostitutes even after the introduction of marriage system. It is said that Satyavati, the unmarried daughter of a fisherman, had sexual relationship with "Parasara" and gave birth to "Vedavyasa" the compilor of *Mahabharata*. Later she became the queen of "Santanu" the great grandfather of the Kauravas and Pandavas.

The Muhammedan noblemen who could afford luxury kept "harems" for their pleasures. But in most cases there was very little difference between the harems and the modern brothels.[6] The only difference being that a harem is for the satisfaction of a singleman, while a brothel is visited by a number of men.[7] The famous Hindi poet Kesavadas, a contemporary of Akbar and Jaganhir, has mentioned the name of Pravin Rai or Rai Pravin an educated and eloquent public woman.[8]

Prostitution as a profession was considered as a social evil and prostitutes were considered as inferior in society since the British period onwards. It was due to the modern industrialisation and urbanisation of society that affected the sex ratio in cities. The labourers, leaving their wives and children in native provinces, moved to the urban areas for work. Within a short period the male population multiplied in the urban areas. It automatically led to the growth of brothels also, to satisfy the urge of males who were away from their homes. Side by side, there was lack of family and social control, more contact between men and women during employment, overcrowding and commercialised recreation including cinemas and dancing hals.

CAUSES OF PROSTITUTION

The social, economic, psychological and such other factors were responsible for the women to take up prostitution. The cheif cause of prostitution was mainly due to two reasons: one is biological and the other is socio-economic.[8] The first one is a calling of nature while the second one is a creation of society.

Sanger, from a study of 2,000 prostitutes has mentioned the following causes which induced women to take up prostitution.[9]

Destitution	525
Inclination	513
Seduced and abandoned	258
Drink and desire for drink	181
Illtreatment by parents, relatives or husbands	164
An easy life	124
Bad company	84
Persuaded by prostitutes	71
700 idle to work	29
Violated	27
Seduced in emigrantship	16
Seduced in emigrant boarding house	8
Total	2000

Some scholars regarded economic cause or poverty as the most important reason for female prostitution. True that the girls of poor parents who are unable to provide the proper physical or moral care for their adolescent daughters and also to maintain themselves, sold their daughters to "dallals" for money. For such women prostitution is the last resort to escape from starvation. According to Bonger both absolute and relative poverty affects sex behaviour.[10] Because of absolute poverty many girls resort to prostitution, in order to live. Relative poverty refers to the lack of many of the small luxuries, to attain which they resort to prostitution. The league of Nations Advisory Committee on social questions also pointed out that poverty, overcrowding and low wages are the contributory causes of prostitution.[11]

But it is difficult to assume that the inability to securse a job alone had driven women to prostitution. If the fundamental problem of female prostitution is an economic, then a question arises, why not so many women become prostitutes, but why so few of them do? At the same time prostitution is so common in highly advanced countries also. There were many other compelling factors that sustain prostitution. They were:

(*i*) *Social Values against Unchastity:*

A raped woman or a woman who had illicit sex experience because of some resons, is often to feel that she had nothing her status and she had to accept whatever came on her way. It is true the society forgives the conduct of such a man, while it is different in the case of woman. Thus the offender escapes, while the victim is punished.

(*ii*) *Ignorance:*

Vice rings operating in large urban areas frequently exploit girls from surrounding rural communities. Often they are lured by offers of employment. It was poor woman, especially widows who have none to support them or are ill-treated by their relative think it as a God send. In time they became reconciled to their fate and became a prostitute.

(*iii*) *Unhappy Marital Relationship:*

Unhappy marital relationship causes many women to resort to prostitution. Indissolvable marriages, espcially when the bride-groom is old or a man of bad character, lead to such an action. The old man by his caressess stimulates the slumbering sexual passion in the girl which he can't satisfy fully. The result was often secret relation with men of young.

(*iv*) *The Hard Hot of Widows*:

Another important factor which increased prostitution was the difficulties on widows to remarry. The widows were sometimes considered as a burden by their relatives. The ill-treatment and the cruelties sometime lead them to leave their homes with men who offers them a life of comfort and luxury.

(*v*) *Inordinate Sex Desire*:

Some girls have uncontrolled sex desires and crave for sex stimulation for its own sake. The desire for new experience either by sex or for the promiscuous social contacts also leads one to prostitution. Some women are by nature easy as well as confort loving. This desire for easy and comfort loving also becomes contributory cause to prostitution. At the same time it is possible that a girl who is addicted to drink also may undergo her first sex experience.

(*vi*) *Vested Interests*:

The highly profitable nature of the business makes many girls to resort to prostitution. Profit motive is the aim of business. In order to attract fresh recruits in the form of young girls, some managers formed organization, the aim of which is to interest young girls in prostitution and to keep them in the business there they have once entered. In a survey of prostitution in Bombay city conducted by S.D. Punekar and Kanlala

Rao, is found that one third of the non-hereditary prostitutes left their homes and entered the brothels under conditions which may be broadly termed as "involuntary", that is due to deception, kidnapping or being forced in to the profession with no choice whatsoever.[12]

Generally we have seen two types of prostitutes (*i*) overt and (*ii*) the clandestine group. The overt group includes professional registered as well as unregistered prostitutes, who generally live in brothel houses.[13] But there are so many girls who are employed in other field of work, especially personal service in other field or as entertainers. Such girls are accustomed to practice of prostitution as a more or less regular supplement to their legitimate earnings. The clandestine prostitutes include a wide variety of women who enter into sex relation with men for mercenary considerations.

LIFE OF PROSTITUTES

For a woman the chastity and faithfulness were considered as the primary virtues. The girls who are born in or brought up to the trade of prostitution can have no choice in life. There is no wonder that the daughter of a prostitute will also naturally lead the life of shame and condemnation from society. If a man had done the same mistake of immorality, there is not mubh response and society pardoned him. But in the case of a woman, she got condemnation from every nook and corner and gradually she lost the contacts from all respectful people. Such a woman thus suffers great personal deterioration. Prof. Reckless has given two stages of maladjustment as an aftermath of unsocial sex activities. The first one is the dual person and the second is the demoralised person.[14] The dual person who lead a double life do not suffer a complete moral collapse in society. But the second type suffered a complete demoralization.

Prostitution is not only a social but also a medical problem. Veneral disease is the common malady of a prostitute. For every night she submitted hereself of men without any discrimination. She thus runs the rick of infection due to the risk of her cohabitation with men. But the bad effect of prostitution not only affects the individual itself, but his or her family also. The married person may get some veneral disease from the prostitute which automatically affect his wife and children. Similarly a married woman who resorts to clandestine prostitution may get the disease from her other client. Prostitution does not exact its full price in social ostracism, shame and stigma. Fully half of those suffering with veneral disease have acquired it through promiscuous sex relationships. The other half are innocent victims—the wives and children of men who acquired disease in premarital or extramarital contacts.[15]

Among the prostitutes even though there are cases of pregnancy, very few have children. The sterility of a prostitute accounting to Santosh Kumar Mukharji may be due to (*i*) veneral disease (*ii*) wild and irregular life and (*iii*) promiscuous intercourse.[16] Besides this they got some other diseases like pthisis gastric derangements, rheumatism and other chromic diseases due to irregular life exposure to the weather, sleepless nights, constant excitement and debauchery, excessive drinking and alternate extremes of want and luxury. As Elliott and Merrill observe, the veneral diseases syphilis, chancroid and gonogrhoea are the vital social concern not only because they are epidemic and devastating diseases but also because they are factors in so many other social problems. Veneral diseases produce a large number of insanity. Children of syphilific parents are apt to be mained for life. Many are born blind. The result of syphilitic and gonorrhoeal infections are so appalling that they rank as major public health problems.[17]

CONTROL OF PROSTITUTION

Various efforts were made in the past to prevent the growth of prostitution through public opinion or by legislation. All Hindu law givers such as Manu, Gautama and Brishaspati recommended for the suppression of prostitution. Gautama Forbade taking meal at the house of a public woman[18] an act which was not formely considered as improper.

During the period of the Mauryans also we find the suppression of brothers. Kautilya, the great politician of Mauryan period, laid down rules for keeping public women under the control.[19] He ordered that "the ganikas[20] were segregated in the southern portion of a town. It is the main duty of the superintendent to warn prostitutes if their expenses be more and think of other possibilities of maintenance if their income be less."

Prostitution was much in vogue during the Muhammedan period also. But Aurangazeb laid down certain rules to suppress prostitution. He ordered that prostitutes and even 'Kanchans' should either marry or else leave the empire.[21] But however the rapid spread of industrialization and urbanization during the British period increased this evil and certain legislative measures were undertaken to prevent it.

Certain regulations dealing with sexual offences were made in the Indian Penal Code, whose object was to protect women against forced sexual intercourse. The code provided an imprisonment up to one year or fine or both for insulting the modesty of any woman by any word, sound gesture or exhibition or any object, or intruding on her privacy. Similarly a penality of two years imprisonment or fine or both was provided for the offence of assault or use of criminal force upon a woman with intent to outrage her modesty.[22]

In order to enquire about the prostitution in the city of Bombay, in 1921 the Government appointed a Commission. The Commission published its report in 1922, recommended the suppression of the brothels containing 5,169 prostitutes.[23] The result was the passing of Bombay Prevention of prostitution Act XI of 1923. But it only recommended for the suppression of male management of brothels. Public opinion arose and the Act was amended in 1926 and again in 1927. But the problem was not solved and the agitation against prostitution still continued.

In Madras the suppression of immoral Traffice Act (Act V of 1930) popularly known as the Brothels Act was passed by the local legislative council.[24] But the act does not allow legislation against third parties. With certain variations similar acts were passed in some other states like Bengal (1933), Uttar Pradesh (1933), Punjab (1935), Bihar (1948), and Madhya Pradesh (1953).

Certain special acts were passed to protect some girls who were engaged in prostitution under certain social customs. Such acts were the U.P. Naik Girls Protection Act (1929), the Bombay Devadasi Protection Act (1934) and the Madras Devadasi (Prevention of Dedication) Act (1947). Under the U.P. Naik Girls Protection Act District Magistrates were empowered to call for particulars from persons having the guardianship or control of Naik Girls under 18 years of age and to restrict or regulate their movements to protect them from being trained to the profession of prostitution and to remove them from immoral surroundings.[25] Under the Devadasi Acts any ceremony or act intended to dedicate a woman as a Devadasi with or without her consent was made illegal act because previously such Devadasis were later on exposed to prostitution as they could not marry.[26]

It was looking to the evil of prostitution which brings in its train personal and community disorganisation, the Moral Hygiene Advisory Committee was appointed in 1954 by the Central Welfare Board of the Govt. of India to study the Proplem of Prostitution. The chairman of the Committee was Mrs. Dhanavanthi Rama Rao.[27] On the lines recommended by the Committee, the Govt. of India passed in Decemper 1956 the suppression of immoral Traffic in Women and Girls Act.

By the act of 1956, not only the keeping of brothels and procuring and living on the earnings of prostitutes is illegal put both the prostitutes and person with whom such prostitution is carried on within a distance of two hundred yards from any public place are punishable. The magistrates were also empowered to remove prostitutes from any place, which they considered harmful to the public. But inspite of all the measures the commercialized vice of sex selling continued in full vigour in the industrial and urban centres. Nobody is unkown that G.B. Road is Delhi's red light area or that there are cages in Bombay where we can buy the favours of girls, some of whom may be barely 12 years old. As Kingsley Davis argued that it is because in unorganised sex trade, the seller, manager and worker are all one and the same woman and obiviously it cannot be eliminated.[28]

Thus the suppression of Immoral Traffic in women and girls Act, 1956 is one of the most hypocritical useless pieces of legislation, yet not a single women's group has been agitated for its repeal.[29] The failure of the law is that the women who end their life in brothels are generally illiterate and ignorant of their rights. They came in the brothels because they are either abandoned by their husbands or they came from poor families or that a female relative sells them into the trade merely to avoid of paying a dowry to marry them. The commercialised society's attitude about a prostitute is that it never accepts her back as respectful human being. Men of conventional society refuses to marry "once a prostitute girl". The Advisory Committee on Social and Moral Hygine observed, "The question of exploitation of women and girls generally is so closely linked with prostitution that it is impossible to suggest measures to wipe out the one without taking into consideration the other.[30]

MEASURES TO REMOVE PROSTITUTION

(*a*) *Sexual Education*

For the better future of the well being of the girls, they should be educated as to the dangers of venereal diseases from their mothers and teachers. The right attitude towards sex are inculcated right from the beginning, then it would be treated by every one as a normal, natural healthy phenomenon rather than as a dirty and sinful things to be obssessed with all the time.

(*b*) *Employment opportunities to women*

There should be more employment opportunities for the girls who were compelled to prostitution to some extent, due to economic problems. So useful employment of girls automatically reduced the number of cases.

(*c*) *Special information about venereal diseases*

Information about venareal diseases should be propagated by means of lectures, films etc. and should be issued in bulletins and pamphlets in order to make the pepole aware of its ocnsequences. At the same time if a prostitute is suspected to become infected, it is her duty to avoid her connection with anybody. At the same time she must inform it to her keep or for immediate curing.

(*d*) *Encouraged widow remarriage*

In some communities the wodows were strictly prohibited to take part in important ceremonies or functions and they lead a secluded life. But there are some widows who cannot live up to this life. They came out from the shell of orthodoxy and a slip from the path of vertue. So to avoid prostitution widow remarriage should be encouraged and child marriage prevented.

The western education and western science had a great influence upon the life of the people of the East particularly the position of women. The presence of fallen women is a blot in the name of the fair sex. "They do not minister simply to lust, what they sell and give in the bargains is much more than that, it is womanhod"[31]. As woman is the backbone of national development, and family is the first school, the core of development is only through the hands of woman. Moreover, today's children are tomorrow's citizens, so mothers are the real agents of development. Hence this is the right time to gather woman and to challenge against prostitution. The elite women undoubtedly formed an important agent against the traffic, in human bodies.

BIBLIOGRAPHY

Biswanath Joardar, *Prostitution in Historical and Modern Perspectives,* Inter India Publications, New Delhi, 1984.

Elliot M.A. and Merril F.E. *Social Disorganisation,* Harper Brothers Publishers, Newyork, 1961.

Gautama, Chapter 17. Geoggrey, May, 'Prostitution' an *Encyclopeadia of Social Sciences,*Vol. XII, 1935.

Kautilaya, *Arthasastra,* 11, Chapter 28.

League of Nations Advisory Committee on Social Questions, Enquiry into Measures of Rehabilitation of Prostitutes, 1938.

Madan C.R. *Indian social problems, social disorganisation and Reconstruction* Vol. I Third Edition, Allied Publishers, New Delhi 1981.

Punekar, S.D. and Kamala Rao, *A Study of the Prostitutes in Bombay: with special reference to family background,* Lalvani Publishing House, Second Edition, 1967.

Reckless, Walter C. "Vice and person disorganisation", *Journal of Applied Sociology*, December 1920.

Report of the Advisory Committee and Social and Moral Hygiene, Central Social Welfare Board, Govt. of India, Arjuna Press, New Delhi, 1954.

Robert K. Merton and Robert A. Nisbet, *Prostitution in Contemporary Social Problems* (ed) Newyork.

Sanger, W.A. *History of Prostitution,* Medical Publishing Company, Newyork.

Mukherji, Santosh Kumar, *Prostitution in India*, Inter India Publications, New Delhi 1987.

Bhattacherji, Sukumari, "Prostitution in Ancient India", *Social Scientist*, Vol 15, No. 2, Feb. 1986.

Tavleen, "A Case for Freeing Prostitutes from the Clutches of Police", *Manushi*, Vol. 5, No. 27, March-April 1985.

Wells, H.G., *The Work, Wealth and Happiness.*

REFERENCES

1. Madan, C.R. *Indian Social Problems, Social Disorganisation and Reconstruction*, Vol. I, Third Edn. Allied Publishers Private Limited, New Delhi, 1981, p.200.
2. Geoffrew, May, "Prostitution" in *Encyclopaedia of social sciences* Vol. XII (1935) p.553.
3. Madan, C.R. *op.cit*, p.200.
4. Bhattacharji, "Prostitution in Ancient India", *Social Scientists*, Vol. 15, No. 2, (February 1987) pp. 132-157.
5. Kautilya's *Arthasastra*, V. 195, 18-19.
6. Brothel means any house, room or place which the occupier or person in charge thereof habitually allows to be used by any other person for the purpose of prostitution.
7. Mukherji, Santosh Kumar, *Prostitution in India*, Inter India Publications, New Delhi, 1986, p.65.
8. Madan, C.R. *op.cit;* p.201.

9. Sanger, W.A. *History of Prostitution*, Medical Publicity Company, New York, p.448.
10. Bonger, W.A. *Criminality and Economic Condition*, 1916, pp.321-56.
11. League of Nations Advisory Committee on Social Questions, Enquiry in to Measures of Rehabilitation of Prostitutes, 1938, p.7.
12. Punekar, S.D. and Kamala Rao, *A Study of the Prostitutes in Bombay—with special reference to family background*, Lalvani Publishing House, Second edn. 1967, p.103.
13. Madan, C.R. *op. cit.*, p. 206.
14. Reckless, Walter C. "Vice and Personal Disorganization." *Journal of Applied Sociology*, Dec. 1926, pp. 134-38.
15. Elliot, M.A. and Merrill, F.E. *Social Disorganisation*, Harper Brothcrs Publishers, New York, 1961, p. 264.
16. Mukharji, Santosh Kumar, pp.266-67.
17. Elliott, M.A. and Merrill F.E. *op. cit.*, p. 265.
18. Gautama, Chapter 17.
19. Kautilya, *Arthasastra* 2, Chapter. 28
20. The designation of Ganika was the highest and had to be earned through beauty, charm and accomplishments, it signified the highest social class among the prostitutes, *Kamasutra*, 11, 27.
21. Biwanath Joardar, *op. cit.* p. 49
22. Section 354.
23. Mukherji, Santosh Kumar, *op. cit.*, p.463.
24. *Ibid.*, p.464.
25. Madan, C.R., *op. cit.*, p. 212.
26. *Ibid.*
27. Biswanath Joardar, *Op. cit.* p. 4.
28. Robert K. Merton and Robert A. Nisbet, *Prostitution in Contemporary Social Problems*, (ed) Newyork, 1963, p. 280.
29. Tavleen Singh, "A case for Freeing Prostitutes from the clutches of Police', *Manushi*, Vol. 5, No. 27, March-April, 1985) pp.2-4.
30. Report of the Advisory Committee on Social and Moral Hygiene, Central Social Welfare Board, Govt. of India, Arjun Printers, New Delhi 1954, p.17.
31. Wells, H.G. *The Work, Wealth and Happiness of Mankind*, p.545.

11

WOMEN AND RURAL DEVELOPMENT: THE INDIAN EXPERIENCE—AN OVERVIEW

DR M. INDIRA DEVI

RURAL Development is viewed as a complex process of change in rural sub-systems and their interaction leading to desired improvements in rural incomes, employment opportunities, income distribution and other aspects of rural life. In all these activities, women who constitute half of the total strength are involved either as partners in bringing about change or as beneficiaries of these. As such, women also should be considered as the core of the rural development strategy, in in view of their key roles as producers and as deliverers of basic needs, apart from concern with inequality, discrimination and the status of women. However, while rural development policies and strategies demand a great deal from women, in production, in family care, their access to knowledge, resources and decisions, which would enable them to perform these roles adequately has not received due attention, except in the recent past (Ahmad, Z. and Martha, F. 1984, 5). In view of their strength and participation in most of the rural development activities, their involvement and integration in development is vital towards eradication of problems of poverty, economic and social success (Devadas, P.R., 1977, 92).

Since the beginning of the UN decade for women, attention has been focussed on the role of rural women in development. However, it is said that like development in general, rural development is also regressive in effect in relation to women.[1] As the UN decade for women has been over, it is pertinent to look into the Indian experience in involving and integrating women in rural development. This article is divided into three sections. Section I deals with the role of rural women on the economic and social front with focus on the Indian scene. Section II examines the strategies considered appropriate for integration of women in rural development, and an overview of the efforts at integrating women in development in the post-independent era are dealt with in Section III.

SECTION I

Women constitute nearly half of the work force in the rural areas in the developing countries though their contribution to economic and social development remained largely invisible (Safilios-Rothschild, 1985, 299; Wilson., 1985, 1019). The issue has attracted attention in the world at large (Leghorn and Parker, 1981, 51). A perceptive understanding of women rural economic activity is necessary to evaluate the strategth aimed at involving women in rural development and their outcomes (Hunlington S., 1975, 1012). Women's activities are broadly divided into three categories (a) Income producing, (b) Income-substituting, and (c) Home-making and child care (Tinker and Cho, 1981, 345). To this one must add an important activity like participation in decision making.

INCOME-PRODUC INGACTIVITIES

In developing countries[2] like India, where around 40.4 per cent (Government of India, 1985, 4) are living below poverty line, a vast majority are directly engaged in the Income producing activities. As per the NSS 32nd Round, the work participation rate of females in the age group of 15-59 in 1985 is estimated as 76.20 per cent. Research in the area suggests, that, within the given socio-cultural milieu "highest female participation rates are observed among the poorest families" (Parthasarathy, G., and Dasaradha Rama Rao, G., 1981, 125; Deere, 1982, 805). These pertain to areas like working as wage labour in the hired market. In addition to these groups, a sizeable proportion of women belonging to the small and marginal farm households,[3] also directly participate in Income-producing activities like work on family farm, hired labour and looking after cattle etc., though in a heirarcical society like India social practices based on caste, restrain some to work outside the home (Sharma, Miriam; Indira Devi, M., 1983, 16).

INCOME-SUBSTITUTING OR COST-SAVING ACTIVITIES

Majority of the rural women, with the marginal exceptions of the rich and the higher caste groups, participate in Income-substituting activities or to put appropriately in cost-saving activities. For example, those belonging to the poorer strata, particularly the landless spend considerable amount of time in fetching water, collecting fuel, processing grain, sewing clothes, repairs to houses, caring for small animals and poultry.[4] On the other hand, those belonging to farm households spend considerable time in activities like cleaning, drying and processing the grain for seed in the farm in addition to requirements of family consuption, kitchen gardens, dairying and poultry activities. However, this type of contribution continued to be considered invisible, as none of these are treated as work by most of the economists and statisticians.

HOME MAKING AND CHILDCARE

While participating in labour force, women alone have to share the burden of home-making and childcare particularly in countries like India where the sexual division of labour is such that women's roles centre round hearth (Dube, S.C., 1955, 170). Case studies conducted in various developing contries including India as part of the inter-regional ILO project on 'Energy and Rural Women's Work' confiirm that rural women tend to work longer hours than men over all, with abcut half of their working hours devoted to essential survival tasks such as fetching fuel and water, cooking and childcare which are not generally considered 'productive labour' (Ahmad and Martha F., 1984, 50-51). A time-disposition study on work participation by landless poor revealed that the average number of work hours per day varied from 15.00 to 18.07 hours and the time spent on domestic work alone is more than 8 hours excluding child care (Indira Devi, M., 1983, 11).

Thus women as care takers of the home spend more than an 8 hour work day with little or no financial reward, a thankless job for many women.

DECISION-MAKING

Though in a patriachal setting, even if the final say in many matters rests with the husband women do participate and contribute to the decision-making process. In a study on 'Interpersonal family it is observed that in relationships in Hindu nuclear families both in the rural and urban areas, the husband is compelled to turn to his wife and implicitly she becomes a partner in his decisions (Narain Dheerendra, 1970, 461). A recent study on Role of Farm Women in Agriculture (Sisodia, 1985, 226, 267) has sharply focussed on a variety of farm decisions in which wives are being consulted. The study observed that nearly 1/3rd of the farm wives are consulted in matters such as choice of crops to be grown, seeds to be used, fertilizer application, number of irrigations, quantity of grain to be marketed and the place of marketing. The study further noted that the degree of female participation in matters like new ideas in agriculture is inversely related to the social heirarchy of the households. Thus women either as wives or as mothers do play a vital part in decisions of significance to the farm and the home.

SECTION II

Integration of women in rural development came to the fore in the recent past. By and large, the strategies concerned for integrating women in rurral development could be classified into four categories: (1) Education, (2) Extension, (3) Technology and (4) Women's Organisations.

EDUCATION

Meaningful and effective participation of people in any activity, economic or social is possible, only those involved understand and are equipped for the roles expected of them (Sawer J. Barbara., 1973, 417). It is said, that the ability to read and write open for women, new and crucial channels of communication, access to information and greater options in employment (Lisa Leghorn and Parker, 1981, 223). This becomes difficult in the absence of education, exposure and skills. The act, that literacy levels are particularly low among women highlights the significance and relevance of the emphasis laid, in promoting female literacy and education. The significance of this becomes more pronounced in a country like India where about 83 percent of female work force involved in agriculture and related occupations are illiterate (Mukhopadhyay, Swapna, 1981, 96). For example, the literacy rares of rutal women for the country as a whole is 17.96 percent (Seventh Plan 1985, Vol. II, 321). With high degree of illiteracy and enmeshed In customs and traditions of a heirarchical society based on caste, rural women find it difficult, to act as enlightened and effective role-takers and enacters, not only in the production and in the social arena, but also as decision makers and particularly in safeguarding themselves against discrimination, social and economic.

EXTENSION

The involvement of women in income-producing, cost saving unpaid, labour, and home-making and childcare and their participation in decision-making process, though not effectively documented[5], the limited evidence however shows that women had a say in matters of purchase of household articles and equipment compared to farm issues (Dhillon, Gurmeet, 1980, 21). In a recent study Sisodia observed that in joint families not only the wives but also the mothers have a large role in decision-making and the percentage of wives consulted with respect to new ideas in agriculture forms 1/3rd of the sample households and the involvement of women in decision-making is compartively high among backward classes, scheduled castes and scheduled tribes (Sisodia, 1986, 224-225). This implies that modernization through greater acceptability of new ideas, health programmes and family planning measures, becomes possible, only, when the concerned agencies address themselves to the women also. Many studies[6] have focussed attention on the need for greater coverage of women and the neglect of women by these agencies with the possible exception of extension programmes related to health and childcare. Johnston and Clark traced this to predominance of men as agricultural extension agents and due to lack of recognition of the significant involvement in and contribution to production and income-earning activities by women (Johnston and Clark, 1982, 103).

The technologies in relation to women could broadly be divided in two types, those that help to reduce drudgery and the other non-displacing technologies that help income generation improvement of health without displacement of labour.

TECHNOLOGY

The role of technology in relation to rural women came into force, out of concern for rural women in the third world who work hard for long hours for meagre rewards (Palmer Ingrid, 1977, 107), but in societies with high degrees of inequality of income with significant numbers below poverty line evolving appropriate technologies to remove drudgery come into conflict with employment objectives as the technologies emerged so far like the rice-milling resulted in depriving the poor women of employment in such avenues (Agarwal, Bina, 1985, p.161). In this context, labour-intensive technologies, that will not displace labour and removal of imperfections in the rural factor markets through policy measures aimed at structural changes and institutional reforms are highlighted if improved technologies designed for the target group are to reach them in practice (Ahmad Iftikar, 1983, 504).

The crux of the problem of women in relation to technology as observed by Amaryat Sen lies basically in sexual division of labour that force women to less skilled and repetetive jobs and the remedy sought observes Sen 'has to go beyond that of redirecting technological change' (Sen, A.K., 1986, 216). Traditions that discourage women to have access to and use of technology also accounted for these adverse affects. Based on a Kerala study Kala, observed that 'It is almost a taboo for a woman to handle any of the modern labour saving devices and the trend thus indicates adverse effects on female employment due to technological modernization' (Kala, C.V., 1976, 201).

WOMEN'S ORGANIZATIONS

Development literature has often highlighted the organizations of the beneficiaries, for effective implementation of the programmes meant for target groups. Rural women's organizations are considered as one of the key variables in redefining women's relation to the process of development (Croll Elizabeth, 1982, 21). The importance of organizations stems from the fact that no person acting alone can accomplish much. The need for such organizations for women, who need knowledge, material protection and other resources which lie beyond their grasp as individuals, is vital to accelerate their involvement in rural development, particularly in societies where tradition and customs are adverse to women's interaction with outside world. It is only through these institutional devices that rural women, like anybody else can have benefit of developmental organizations, that perform tasks, like making claims and choices on the social system, distribution of resources based on priorities, allocating resources, to permit appropriate responses for priority programmes, resource mobilization and resource productivity (Johnston and Clark, 1982, 156-57).

SECTION III

THE INDIAN EXPERIENCE

Since India became independent, the Indian constitution provided for, not only equal rights and privilegs for men and women, but also for making special provisions for women. Keeping this in view, the various Five year plans have focussed attention on women through a set of special programmes, mostly centered around their feminine and child-bearing activities, though aspects like literacy also formed part of these. Since the beginning of the community development programmes of early 1950s and till the end of the Fifth Plan period, though attention was paid for involving women in development activities through organizational devices such a Mahila Mandals, by and large they were not tuned for active participation of women. As the Sixth Plan document admits "despite development measures and the constitutional legal guarantees, women have lagged benind men in almost all sectors" (Sixth Plan, 1980, 423). It is only since the Sixth Plan period an effective beginning has been made towards efforts at involving women in development activity for the first time[7]. The Indian experience is examined against the framework of the strategies commonly suggested for involving women in rural development, viz., education, extension, technology, and women's organisations.

EDUCATION

The low level of literacy i.e., 7.93 percent of female population in 1951 coupled with cognition of the contribution of primary schooling to economic development[8] attracted the attention of the planners and sustained efforts were made to extend facilities for the education of girls since the beginning of the First Five Year Plan itself. These efforts have resulted over time in reducing disparities in enrolment and literacy between boys and girls particularly in the age group of 6-11, though these disparities continued to remain with increase in the age-groups. For example, while the enrolment of rate in the age group of 6-11 increased from 60 percent in 1950-51 to 100 percent by 1980s for boys, it rose from 25 percent to 66 percent for girls during the same period. On the other hand, in the 11-14 age group enrolment rate of boys increased from 21 percent to 70 per cent by 1980 while that of girls rose from 5 to 38 percent only (For details see Appendix-I). The VII Plan also noted that enrolment of girls has been lagging behind despite special measures taken in the past (Seventh Five Year Plan, 1985, Vol. II, 257). Despite progress in the enrolment rate, the comparatively high drop out rate particularly of those belonging to the economically and socially weaker sections, due to compulsions to join labour force at early age or to take care of brothers and sisters and to attend to household chores when parents go out for work among other reasons (Bardhan, K., 1979, V-2), is thwarting efforts at bridging disparities in literacy levels between sexes and between rural and urban areas.

Compared to the progress achieved in eradicating illiteracy, the concern for promoting literacy of the females in the age group 15 and above continues to be limited as the female literacy rate is only 24.9 percent as per 1981 census, while it is much lower at 19.96 percent in rural areas (Sixth Five Year Plan, 1980, 321). This is largely due to the limited success of adult education programmes initiated since 1950s. As the Seventh Plan has rightly perceived, problem of sociological nature like, restriction on girls going out of house after puberty, general restrictions on the newly married daughters-in-law coupled with their multiple roles as daughter-in-law, absence of female instructors to conduct these classes in the rural areas, have mullified the efforts at promoting literacy among the female adults. Taking cognition of these, the Seventh Plan has included adult education as a mojor trust area and aims at involving social institutions, voluntary organizations students, teachers and to link these effectively with various developmental programmes particularly the integrated rural development programme (IRDP). It also plans to ensure active participation of Village Panchayats, Mahila Mandals, Community Centres etc. (Seventh Five year Plan, 1985, Vol. 2, 257-258).

EXTENSION

Since the beginning of Community Development Programme, India has evolved a well knit programme of extension system covering various facets of rural economic activity and societal development through a team of extension officers for agriculture, livestock, cooperatives, industries, education, social education, and women's welfare. Under the leadership of block development officer acting as the coordinator of this team of specialists, the pattern remained more or less the same. However, except in the case of those concerned with women's welfare and health visitors, the rest of the team is partly for want of qualified women. The sex composition of the extension staff coupled with lack of appreciation of women's contribution in agriculture and related activities, resulted in total absence of any exposure of women to the extension system centered round productive activities. The traditional seclusion of women to the unknown and outside males also furthered this process; as a result, most of the women involved in income-producing and income-substituting activities and women-headed households failed to have any access to extension agencies. Moreover, Indian extension system is largely geared towards the producers and among them, the releatively well-off and thus, ignore those participating in the labour force including women. The failure of the system to convince and orient these groups towards new methuds, has resulted in the low acceptability of practices like Japanese Method of Paddy Cultivation (Epstein's 1962, 63-64). Keeping this in view, Rajammal, P. Devadas (1977,93) stressed that extension efforts in agriculture must cater fully to women as lack of comprehension and consequent inability to handle innovations out of ignorance, only results in rejecting innovations by women.

At the village level, workers now styled as village development officers, the multipurpose workers also bypassed women like the extension staff. Their female counterparts called Gramsevikas are not only limited, but also are not oriented towards extension in productive activities as their major focus is towards women's organizations and related welfare tasks.

It is only the women extension officer, with the help of Gramsevikas was incharge of extension activities among women. These are largely oriented to promote group activities through organization of Mahila Mandals and to promote general wakening of women out of subvertion and beliefs, though organization of sewing centres and sex-specific productive activities like hoisery and related crafts are encouraged.

It is only in matters relating to health and sanitation, the extension system representing the health visitors exposed women, in matters of childcare and methods of family planning, with different degrees of success, partly due to the inadequacy of staff, and largely due to ignorance and illiteracy among women who are also constrained by the patriarchal authority and decision-making. This apart, there is general criticism, that as in the case of production-oriented extension agencies, those concerned with health and family welfare have by passed the lower strata of women who are numerically significant, and are exposed to health hazards, out of poverty. In a perceptive article on 'Towards Women's perspective on family planning' Vimal Balasubramanyam observed that the paradox that characterizes family planning in India is, on the one hand women are the major targets of Family Planning programme with both messages and methods be aimed intensively at them, while on the other hand, they felt contraception needs of these target women are not adequately catered to. The women are doubly victimised by the patriarchal family, which refuses to allow them to use contraception and by the population controllers, who make them the targets of unsafe contraception programmes Balasubramanayam, V, 1986, 69).

TECHNOLOGY

The issue of appropriate technology to improve the life and status of women has received attention of the planners particularly since the Sixth Five Year Plan, though some efforts in this direct ion have been initiated, since the beginning of community development in 1950s, like propagation of smokeless chulas to safeguard women's health from the hazards of conventional practices, which expose them to smoke and heat. The

Sixth Five Year Plan observed that application of science and technology to the improvement of the life and status of women will depend upon the development of home technologies, suitable agricultural technologies for improvement of productivity, forestry, sericulture, handloom and crafts like pottery could be considered as potential segments of women's work where application of simple technology can go a long way in improving their productivity and give them enough time to participate in pro grammes for their educational and other development. It also recognized the need for evolving appropriate technologies for both working in small and unorganized sector, particularly those applicable to women facing serious occupational hazards in several professions leading to avoidable health problems and use of mass media for the spread of technologies relevant to home needs, such as care and maintenance of household gadgets (Sixth Five Year Plan, 1980, 323).

The VII Plan emphasized the need for involvement of voluntary agencies, homescience colleges and women workers at all levels. However, these two documents not even the Seventh Plan referred to the type of technologies evolved either to remove drudgery or to prevent occupational hazards.

While not much is known about the appropriate technologies that have come into being, since the Sixth Plan period, like mechanization has hit women's employment in post-harvest operations in rice areas, where grinding, hand pounding, separating and cleaning—all women's occupations. Saradhi Acharya observed that a typical rice mill in Western India displaces about 1500 women's jobs and creates about 45 jobs for men (Acharya, S,1984,95-6). Brandtzaeg observed that even in the case of the commercial crops technology had the effect of increasing women's work burden. Similar effects are noted in respect of dairy and fisheries. Though, traditionally, dairy activities were in the hands of women specially of the poorer castes, the advancement as well as benefits out of dairy. Similar trends are noted in respect of fishery where women have lost their contral over preservation and marketing of fish to big business houses with the emergence of new technologies and take over of these by men (Brandtzaeg, B., 1979, 1921-22).

In the case of energy also, it was observed that the emergence of bio-gas plants resulted in deprivation of poor households dependent on free supply of dung as these measures are not backed by significant progress in the direction of social forestry to meet the domestic fuel needs of the community (Nagabrahman and Shareekat Sambrani, 1983, 38). It was also noted that the use of bio-gas for rural industrial development as agronds of viability of existing bio-gas plants adversely affects woman's cooking energy needs (Batliwala, S., 1983, 2229-30).

The labour displacement character of even simple technologies and illiteracy and poverty of the rural masses is also a stumbling block in evolving and spread of technologies aimted at improving directivity and removal of drudgery. The limited efforts in this direction have helped, to relieve drudgery of women belonging to richer strata in the urban setting, those of middle class and above.

WOMEN'S ORGANIZATIONS

Indian planners have recognized the need for women's organizations and accordingly Mahila Mandals were organized since the beginning of the community development programme. These organizations are floated at the village level, though their number varied from block to block. The programmes drawn for women by these organizations included crafts and cottage industries, maternity and child welfare, Bhajans (Prayers) and discussions, demonstrations and exhibitions related to food and health, literacy and education, kitchen gardens and pits compost, care of cattle and poultry (Das Parimal., 1959, 33-34). The programmes listed above are ideal in character and the sociological problems that hindered adult literacy programmes for women also stood in the way of mass participation of women in these organizations and much less by those from the weaker sections. As a result, these organizations have remained or confined to elitist groups in the rural areas centered round leisure-time activities, thus contributing if any, marginally, to improve productivity or to promote awakening on the parts of the vast majority of illiterate women. A study in late 1970s by Jain and Krishna Murthy Reddy showed that though Mahila Mandals acted as a forum for involvement of women in development of women in develp-mental activity at the village level, they suffer from many limitations. These organizations depended on individual leader-ship without any organized pattern of functioning and the activities centered round nutrition, child care, tailoring and these organizations are dominated by 'higher echelons' of society in terms of caste, occupation and financial status. They further observed, that, there is poor representation of weaker sections for whom the activities of Mahila Mandals have no relevance. They also noted that there is an excessive dependence on Government (Jain and Reddy, 1977, 93) grants and the absence of drive to raise funds locally. Though the study is limited to a region, the findings are applicable equally well, to the current status of activities of these organizations at the village level in other regions as well.

To sum up, the Indian experience in integrating women in rural development has not met withe great success. There is limited recognition of the contribution of women to rural development, till the commencement of the women's deve-lopment decade. Further, other welfare oriented programmes also have received a setback partly due to illiteracy of women themselves, the paucity of trained women personal to men thoes programmes and also due to the lop-sided implementation of these programmes without effective monitoring. The heirarchical social system, that doesn't help all women to come together, patriar chal authority that leaves little discretion to women in matters of decision making and the social values that discourage inter-action with outside world by women on their own and the value that whatever a woman is her ultimate position centres round home and hearth have also contributed to the limited success of efforts at integrating middle class women in rural development in the post-independent India.

In the case of working class woman, though they go out for work along side males and to some extent also get exposed to influences along with males, poverty, illiteracy and consequent marginalization, mostly accounts for non-integration of these groups in the developmental proces in the countryside.

It is true that some of these problems could be seen as part of the problems of poverty and are not exclusive to women but, what needs to be recognized is the fact that benefits of development failed to percolate to women despite, rise in per capita incomes or special measures to improve the lot of the low income households (Lele Uma., 1986, 215). Amartya Sen and Sunil Sen Gupta's study on Malnutrition of Rural Children affirm this. This study sharply focussed on the sex bias in the economic benefits accruing to children through distribution of land to landless in Bengali village. They observed that "Increasing the income of the rural family my be inadequate instrument in combating the unequal deprivation of the female child" (Sen and Gupta, 1983, 863).

Effective integration of women in development calls for a change in perception from viewing families as interpersonal units to one of looking at these as units in the broad stratification system (Oppenheimer, V.K. 404). It must also be recognised that special efforts are required for transformation of women in the reral areas particularly these belonging to the middle and lower classes.

Great stress must be laid in eradicating female illiteracy and in imparting skills through vocational, to enable them, to accept and handle technological innovations and thus, to avert deprivation due to change in technology. Amartya Sen rightly observed, that women's concentration in low paid jobs is due to disadvantages in education, training and skill formation and policy responses must initiate steps that facilitate job acquisition and removal of discrimination in employment and wage (Sen, A.K., 1986, 216).

Finally, revitalization of the Mahila Mandals, with broad-based membership for middle and poorer strata of women is vital to provide the requisite organizational strength to ensure their due share in the developmental programes and to putforth their voice in demanding a better deal for them. In this process and in evolving appropriate technologies, involvement of women scientists and voluntary organizations will go a long way in eliminating sex biases entrenched in tradition which are stifling efforts at integration of women in rural development, apart from other limitations of the programmes and policies.

NOTES

1. (i) In her Introduction to 'Role of Women in Development,' Vina Majundar observed that most developing countries have undertaken multiple programmes for rural development but the unwitting effect of these appears to distribute the benefits unevenly and often increase inequality between different sections of the population and between men and women. Programmes for women have been marginal in economic development activities initiated in agriculture, animal husbandry, handicrafts, small scale industry, and fisheries, social welfare services, nutrition, childcare and family planning, appear to be offered to rural women as some sort of compensation for the lack of attention given to them to increase their productivity and income earning capacity (Majundar, Vina, 1978, 4).

   (ii) See also Boserup, 1970.

   (iii) Lakshmi Devi Achanti, 1982, 18.

2. Safilos-Rothschild observed that 'In developing countries, all members of low-income families are drawn into the struggle for survival, since no source of income is adequate' (Safilos Rothschild, 1984, 47).
3. A recent study on Female labour participation in rice farming in Chattisgarh region by Marothia and Sharma showed that females contributed a higher proportion of labour input in paddy production activities on all farm size groups (Marothia, D.K. and Sharma, S.K., 1985, 237).
4. Marotha and Sharma observed that on an average female labour spent 60 per cent of their time in subsidiary activities as against 40 per cent by males and their share was highest in fodder collecting activities and preparation of farmyard manure among all size groups (*Ibid.*, 239).
5. In the Indian context, there is very little documentation on the decision-making process in the rural household and much less about areas concerned.
6. See, also Ruth B. Dixon, 1978, 53-54 and Vina Majundar, 1978, 23; Rajammal, P. Devadas, 1977, 93; Suryawanshi and Kapase, 1985, 244.
7. For the first time, the Sixth Five Year Plan has devoted a chapter to women and development and this is being continued in the Seventh Plan also.
8. (i) J.P. Naik observed that 'The relationship between education and society is dialectic social change is necessarily reflected in education and educational changes can prepare the ground for consolidate and complete social changes. The educational

system cannot remain a silent spectator of the social and economic transformation that is taking place and will take place in the world; it has a positive role to play in the creation of the international economic order which visualizes greater equality between and within nations. In this regard, it is worth mentioning that universal elementary education is and egalitarian programme' (1979, 73).

(ii) Christopher Colclough in his review on 'The impact of primary schooling on economic development' observes that primary schooling increases labour productivity in both urban and rural sectors and that the economic returns to such investment are typically high. In addition, it reduces fertility, improves health and nutrition and promotes other behavioural and attitudinal changes which are helpful to economic development. Investment strategies which give primary schooling an important place would be more conducive of growth-with-equity than many alternatives (1988, 181).

APPENDIX I

ENROLMENT OF CHILDREN IN PRIMARY AND SECONDARY EDUCATION BY AGE GROUP AND SEX

Percentage of Pupils in the age group

Year	*6—11*		*11—14*		*6—14*	
	Boys	*Girls*	*Boys*	*Girls*	*Boys*	*Girls*
1950-51	60.0	25.0	21.0	5.0	46.0	18.0
1955-56	70.0	32.0	26.0	7.0	55.0	24.0
1960-61	83.0	41.0	33.0	11.0	65.0	31.0
1965-66	95.0	55.0	44.0	17.0	77.0	42.0
1968-69	96.0	59.0	47.0	20.0	79.0	46.0
1973-74	98.0	78.0	55.0	29.0	84.0	57.0
1979-80*	100.0	66.0	52.0	28.0	82.0	52.0
1984-85**	118.0	69.0	70.0	38.0	91.0	64.0
1989-90**	110.0	88.0	93.0	65.0	104.0	80.0

Source :

1950-56	Third Five Year Plan, 1961, 580-581
1960-69 & 1973-74	Fourth Plan, 1969, 280 & 299
1979-80	Sixth Plan, 1980, 363-365
1984-85 & 1989-90	Seventh Plan, 1985, Vol. II, 265

* Likely enrolment in VII Plan

** Projected enrolment in VII Plan.

REFERENCES

Acharya, S., (1984), Women and Rural Development in the Third World. Paper presented at Workshop on Women, Technology and Forms of Production held at Madras Institute of Development Studies, Madras, October.

Agarwal, Bina, (1985), "Work Participation of Rural Women in Third World: Some Data and Conceptual Biases," *Economic and Political Weekly*, A 155-A 164.

Ahmad, Iftikar., (1983), "Technology and Rural Women in the Third World," *International Labour Review*, 493-505.

Ahmad, Z.M. and Martha F. Loutfi, (1984), "Women Workers in Rural Development," A Programme of the I.O. Rural Employment Policies Branch, Employment and Development Department, ILO GENEVA.

Anker, Richard (1983), "Female Labour Force Participation in Developing Countries: A Critic of Current Definitions and Data Collection Methods," *International Labour Review*, 709-724.

Avinashalingam, T.S. (ed), 'Eradication of Rural Poverty,' Sri Ramakrishna Mission Vidyalaya, Coimbattore, 1977.

Balasubrahmanyam, Vimal (1986), "Towards a Women's Perspective on Family Planning," *Economic and Political Weekly*, 69-71.

Bardhan K., (1979), 'Work as a medium of Earning and Social Differentiation: Rural Women of West Bengal,' Paper presented at A.D.C.—ICRISAT Conference on Adjustment Mechanism of Rural Labour Markets in Developing Areas, Hyderabad, August 22-24.

Batliwala, Srilatha (1983), 'Women in Cooking Energy,' *Economic and Political Weekly*, 227-30.

Boserap, Ester (1970), 'Women's Role in Economic Development,' St. Martin's Press, New York.

Brandtzaeg Brita, (1979), 'Women, Food and Technology—Case of India,' *Economic and Political Weekly*, 1921-24.

Chariton, Sue Ellon M. (ed), 'Women in Third World Development,' Westerview Press, London, 1984.

Christopher Colclough (1982), 'The Impact of Primary Schooling on Economic Development: A Review of the Evidence,' *World Development*, 167-185.

Croll, Elizebeth (1982), Rural Women's Organizations, ILO (ed) Rural Women Workers in Asia.

Das, Parimal, (1959), "Women Under India's Community Development Programme," *International Labour Review*, (July-December), 27-45.

Deere, Carmen Diana, (1982). "The Division of Labour by Sex in Agriculture: A Peruvian Case Study," *Economic Development and Cultural Change*, 795-811.

Devadas, P. Rajammal (1977), "Role of Women in Agricultural Productivity and Home Improvement," in Avinashlingam, T.S. (ed) Eradication of Rural Poverty.

Dhillon, Gurmeet, (1980), "Rural Women in Decision-Making Action," *Kurukshetra*, 19-21.

Dixon, Ruth B., (1978), "Rural Women at Work-Strategies for Development in South Asia," John Hopkins University Press, London.

Dube, S.C., (1955), Indian Village. Routledge and Kegan Paul, London.

Epistein, Scarlet, (1962), "Economic Development and Social Change in South India," Oxford University Press, India.

Government of India (1980), Planning Commission, Sixth Five Year Plan, New Delhi.

——(1985), Seventh Five Year Plan 1985-90.

Huntington, Suellen (1975), "Issues in Women's Role in Economic Development: Critic and Alternatives," *Journal of Marriage and Family*, 1001-12.

Indira Devi, M., "Caste and Women's Participation in Labour Markets: A Study of Landless Poor," Paper presented at the II National Conference on Women's Studies, Trivandrum.

ILO—ARTEP (1981), Women in the Indian Labour Force, Bangkok,

ILO—(1982), Rural Women Workers in Asia, Geneva.

Jain, S.P., and Krishna Murthy Reddy, V., (1977), "Role of Women in Rural Development (A Study of Mahila Mandals), National Institute of Rural Development, Hyderabad.

Johnston Bruce F., and William, C. Clark, (1982), "Redesigning Rural Development—A Strategic Perspective," The John Hopkins University Press, London, 102-104.

Kala, C.V., (1976), 'Female Participation in Farm Work in Central Kerala,' *Sociological Bulletin*, 185-206.

Lakshmi Devi Achanti., (1982), "Role of Rural Women in Agricultural Development," *Kurukshetra*, 15-20.

Lee, Man-Gap (ed), Towards a New Community Life—Reports of International Research Seminar on the Saemaul Movement, Institute of Samaeul Undong Studies, Seoul National University, Seoul, 1981.

Lele, Uma, (1986), 'Women and Structural Transformation—*Economic Development and Cultural Change*, 195-222.

Lisa Leghorn and Parker Catherine, (1981), "Women's Worth: Sexual Economics and the World of Women," Routledge and Kegan Paul, London.

Majundar, Vina, (1978), "Role of Rural Women in Development," Allied Publishing Pvt. Ltd., Bombay.

Marothia D.K., and Sharma, S.K., (1985), 'Female Labour Participation in Rice Farming Systems of Chattisgarh Region,' *Indian Journal of Agricultural Economics*, 235-39.

Mukhopadhyay, Swapna, (1981), "Women Workers of India: A Case of

Market Segmentation," ILO-ARTEP, Women in the Indian Labour Force.

Nagabrahman, D. and Sambrani, Sreekanth., (1983), 'Women's Drudgery in Firewood Collection,' *Economic and Political Weekly* 33-38.

Naik, J.P., (1983), "Relevance of Education to Development Especially in Rural Areas in Education and New International Order," Concept Publishing House, New Delhi.

Narain, Dheerendra, (1970), "Interpersonal relationship in Hindu Family," in Reuben Hill and Rene Konig (ed.), Families in the East and West Paris, The Hague Monton and Co.

Oppenheimer Valerie. Kincade, (1977), The Sociology of Women's Economic Role in the Family, *American Sociological Review*, 387-406.

Palmer, Ingrid, (1977), "Rural Women and the Basic Needs Approach to Development," *International Labour Review*, 97-107.

Parthasarathy, G., and Dasaratharama Rao, G., (1981), "Women in Indian Labour Force," ILO-ARTEP (ed.), Bangkok, 121-37.

Rolthschild, Constantina Safilios, (1984), "The Role of the Family in Development," in Sue Ellen M. Chariton (ed.), "Women in Third World Development."

——., (1985), "The Persistence of Women's Invisibility in Agriculture: Theoritical and Policy Lessons from Lesotho and Sierra Leone," *Economic Development and Cultural Change*, 299.

Sawer J. Barbara., (1973), "Predictors of the Farm Wife's Involvement in General Management and Adoption Decisions," *Rural Sociology*, 412-426.

Sen, A.K., (1986), Women, Technology and Sexual Divisions, UNCTAD, Trade and Development, 195-223.

Sen, A.K., and S. Sengupta, (1983), 'Malnutrition of Rural Children and the Sex Bias,' *Economic and Political Weekly*, 855-864.

Sharma, Miriam, (1985), "Caste, Class and Gender Production and Reproduction in Rural North India," *The Journal of Peasant Studies*, 57-88.

Sisodia, J.S., (1985), "Role of Farm Women in Agriculture: A Study of Chambal Command Area of Madhya Pradesh," *Indian Journal of Agricultural Economics*, 223-230.

Suryawanshi, S.D., and Kapase, K.M., (1985), "Impact of Ghat Irrigation Project on Employment of Female Agricultural Labour," *Indian Journal of Agricultural Economics*, 240-244.

Tinker Irene and Cho Hyoung, (1981), "Women's Participation in Community Development of Korea," in Man-Gap Lee., (ed) Towards a New Comm nity Life., 343-386.

Wilson Fiona., (1985), "Women and Agricultural Change in Latin America: Some Concepts Guiding Research," *World Development*, 1017-1035.

INDEX